# 1 - 2 - 3
# COOK

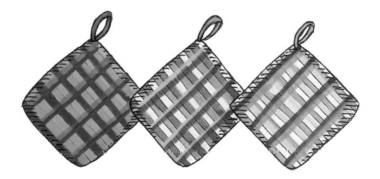

**I dedicate this book to Michael, my mum, and my dad's loving memory. – R. G.**

**To my father, who taught his children that cooking is a fine art. – S. P.**

First published in Great Britain in 2006 by Bloomsbury Publishing Plc
36 Soho Square, London, W1D 3QY

Text copyright © 2006 by Rozanne Gold
Illustration copyright © 2006 by Sara Pinto
The moral rights of the author and illustrator have been asserted

Book design by Sue Schlabach

A CIP catalogue record of this book is available from the British Library

ISBN: 0 7475 8393 5
ISBN-13: 9780747583936

All papers used by Bloomsbury Publishing are natural, recyclable products made from wood grown in
well-managed forests. The manufacturing processes conform to the environmental regulations of the country of origin.

Printed in China

1 3 5 7 9 10 8 6 4 2

www.bloomsbury.com/childrens

**Note about this book:**
As with almost any cookbook, this one includes recipes that require cooking with
heat, and cutting with sharp implements including knives and graters. Any child in a
kitchen should be supervised by a parent or guardian. The creators of this
cookbook take no responsibility for unsupervised cooking by a child, but
have included guidelines for safer cooking.

# 1 - 2 - 3
# COOK

### Cooking with kids using
### only 3 ingredients

## BY ROZANNE GOLD

## Illustrated by Sara Pinto

BLOOMSBURY
CHILDREN'S
BOOKS

chef's hat (not required)

# Contents

# Introduction

My MOTHER TOLD ME THAT that when I was young, I carried a cookbook around with me like a security blanket. I was never without it. I read it in the bathroom, tucked it under my pillow and, of course, brought it to the kitchen!

I adored watching my dad as he stirred gherkin relish into the yummy tuna salad that he always made in a big wooden bowl (see page 56) and I often helped my mother prepare my favourite comfort foods, including buttered noodles with cinnamon sugar (see page 76).

Cooking with friends was always fun. I had an older pal from camp named Mim who loved to bake. One day she came to my house and taught me how to make biscuits. She served them warm with homemade butter (see page 43) that came together in front of my eyes. It was amazing!

Later in life, I became a professional chef. I helped to create some of the world's most magical restaurants and once cooked for a president and a prime minister. (Who knew where my food obsession would lead?)

Cooking always had a special place in my day . . . and in my heart. In the kitchen, there was always time for laughter, learning and sharing.

Cooking can be as easy as 1-2-3. And it should be! Especially if you're just learning how. The recipes contained in this book are very special because they each have only 3 ingredients! A kind of magic occurs when three simple ingredients are transformed into delicious, easy-to-prepare recipes. When you cook your way through this book, you will begin to feel confident in the kitchen. You'll be eager to help get dinner on the table, pack your own lunch, make breakfast in bed for your mother or plan a holiday menu. You also might start creating three-ingredient recipes of your own.

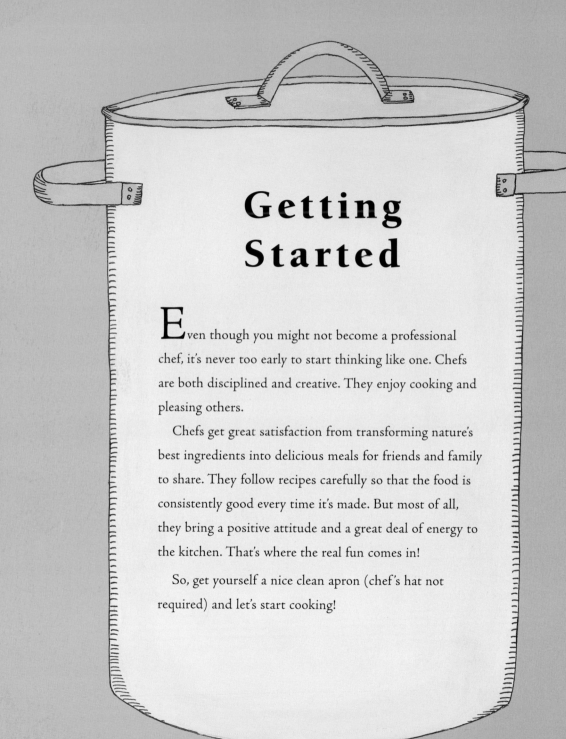

# Getting Started

Even though you might not become a professional chef, it's never too early to start thinking like one. Chefs are both disciplined and creative. They enjoy cooking and pleasing others.

Chefs get great satisfaction from transforming nature's best ingredients into delicious meals for friends and family to share. They follow recipes carefully so that the food is consistently good every time it's made. But most of all, they bring a positive attitude and a great deal of energy to the kitchen. That's where the real fun comes in!

So, get yourself a nice clean apron (chef's hat not required) and let's start cooking!

# Kitchen Basics

You don't need a fancy kitchen to get started. What you do need is a clean surface on which to work, a hob (either gas or electric), an oven and a grill. A toaster is also helpful, especially for making quick and healthy snacks after school. You need pots and pans of various sizes (see page 16), bowls, spoons, chopping boards and several knives, which must be handled with care (see page 17).

## Food Safety

First and foremost, it is essential to **wash your hands** hands with soap and warm water and to make sure your work area is very clean before you start cooking. As you handle raw foods, like meat or fish or vegetables, you should wash your hands, and chopping boards, frequently.

Good chefs always **clean up** as they go along. This keeps the dirty things away from the clean things and prevents a mess from building up.

Put fresh ingredients in the **refrigerator** as soon as you purchase them and as soon as you've finished working with them. Let hot ingredients cool to room temperature before refrigerating them. Do not leave food out for longer than a recipe specifies.

Check the **expiry date** on canned and jarred ingredients. Rinse fruit and vegetables very well before using. Smell everything you use. If it smells bad, throw it out!

## Personal Safety

Kitchens can be very safe places to work, if you follow some simple rules. Always wear **sturdy shoes** just in case anything falls near your feet. **Don't wear loose clothing** or wide sleeves: you don't want to get them wet, dirty, or, worst of all, burned! If you have long hair, pull it back. Never use an oven or grill without a parent, older family member or friend. If your parent allows you, you may use the hob on your own.

It's important to go slowly and concentrate. Work on only one step or procedure at a time.

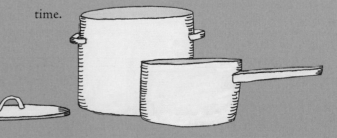

## Danger Zones

Always use **oven gloves** or pot holders to touch **hot pans**. Use knives with care. You might use a small knife after you have gained some confidence and skill. Use large knives with adult supervision. It is important to make sure your knives are **sharp** and in good condition. Dull knives are no good for cutting and can hurt you more often than sharp ones. When you are using a knife, angle it away from you and don't cut towards you or your fingers. Pay attention to where the edge of the blade is at all times and **keep your fingers curled and away from the blade. Do not try to catch a knife if it falls;** rather, quickly step out of the way and pick it up after the fall. Wash it carefully. Store knives on a knife rack or in a knife block.

Be sure to **use the right knife for the right job:** see page 17 for types of knives needed. Always use a **chopping board:** to keep it firmly in place, put a damp kitchen towel or a shallow stack of paper towels underneath.

## Water

Fill saucepans two-thirds full, otherwise they will overflow while you cook, causing burns and making a mess. Be sure to follow the rules of a recipe when it specifies to simmer (small bubbles, low heat), cook over a medium heat or bring to the boil.

## Electricity

Always keep electric appliances away from the sink and any water. Make certain to turn off all electric appliances and sources of heat (oven, hob, etc.) as soon as you finish.

Practise cooking skills and techniques with a parent, or an older family member or friend. If a recipe says to 'do this with an adult', just make sure that you do. Let them show you how to use the blender, food processor, electric mixer or can opener with care.

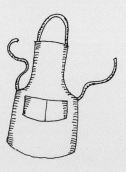

# About the Recipes

The recipes in *1-2-3 Cook* were created and tested by me and then retested by a team of young sous-chefs (assistant chefs). They are Danielle Hartog, aged 10; Robyn Kimmel, aged 8; Ian Kimmel, aged 12; Daniel Glass, aged 11; Sara Rosen, aged 16; Benjamin Deem, aged 10; Max Deem, aged 12; Rachel L. Greenberg, aged 12; Sara Feld, aged 15; Phillip L. Safran, aged 10, Daniel Greenberg, aged 10; Nicholas Green, aged 11. Their feedback and enthusiasm were invaluable to me in choosing which recipes to include.

## The Magic of 1-2-3

When it comes to cooking, three is a magical number. I have found that three ingredients of uncompromising quality are often all you need to create dishes that taste much more delicious than the sum of their parts. The expression 'less is more' works surprisingly well in the culinary arts. Sometimes recipes have *sooo* many ingredients that they become overwhelming.

My 1-2-3 approach is especially appropriate for younger cooks and budding 'gourmets' who basically like simple foods and balanced flavours. Keeping it simple also means you can really focus on what you're doing; it makes cooking more user-friendly, without taking any shortcuts. Three ingredients also means less shopping, less preparation and less cleaning-up, too!

Most magical of all is watching a chocolate cake evolve from a mere trio of ingredients – eggs, chocolate and butter – or an entire meal from just twelve ingredients. No wonder my young sous-chefs had so much fun testing the recipes!

## Flavour and Taste

There are no rights or wrongs in the way we experience taste. Our taste buds are as individual as our fingerprints, and I encourage you to work out for yourself the flavours and dishes you like. And remember this: **your tastes change as you grow older;** something that you dislike today might become your favourite food next year!

When we eat food, we bring all our senses to the table: sight, smell, taste, touch, and even sound (think of the sound a potato chip makes as it goes *c-r-u-n-c-h* in your mouth!). Smell is a very big part of the package: when we smell something delicious, our mouths begin to water and our hunger is stimulated. Or, when we have a cold, it is sometimes hard to taste food because our nose is blocked!

Our sense of taste is complex because it relates to different parts of our brain and nervous system. But it's fun to just think about taste as you cook your way through this book. Good foods are generally a pleasing combination of these flavours: **salty, sour, sweet and bitter**. You might try a dish and say, 'I really like this because it is salty and sweet.' Or, 'I don't like this because it is too sour or bitter.' You might also begin to make small adjustments to my recipes to suit your own taste by adding another pinch of sugar or an extra squeeze of lemon juice.

## How to Follow a Recipe

It is important to read a recipe slowly and carefully all the way through before you get started. This way you will know what ingredients to buy and what utensils you will need. You will also know if you will be needing a hob or other equipment that will require the help of an adult to use.

It's a good idea to **set all your ingredients out in front of you** and prepare them according to the procedures in the recipe. In professional kitchens this is called *mise en place*, which is French for 'everything in its place'. It is important to measure the ingredients carefully and to follow the instructions as they are written – otherwise there is no guarantee that the recipe will turn out well! You will find some helpful cooking terms at the end of this chapter on page 19.

# Measuring

Here are a few important things to know for measuring ingredients correctly in a recipe.

You can get measuring spoons in different sizes. For these recipes, it is useful to have:

| | |
|---|---|
| $1/4$ teaspoon | 1 teaspoon |
| $1/2$ teaspoon | 1 tablespoon |

**Anytime that you are trying a recipe for the first time, or one that uses a cooker, knives or electrical appliances, please be sure you have a parent, older family member or friend to help you.**

If you don't have measuring spoons then you can guess using an actual teaspoon or tablespoon! And if you don't have a tablespoon, it is worth knowing that 3 teaspoons = 1 tablespoon! When using measuring spoons, level off the ingredients with the straight edge of a blunt knife.

You will also need a measuring jug, usually made out of glass or plastic. This is for measuring liquids, and here they are measured in metric units of litres and millilitres (ml). There are 1,000 ml in a litre. Imperial units of fluid ounces (fl oz) and pints are also given.

For measuring all other ingredients, you need a set of kitchen scales to weigh them. If you need to measure an ingredient in a bowl, make sure you put the bowl on the scales first and set the scales to 0 before adding the ingredient. Solid ingredients are measured here in grams (g) and kilograms (kg). However, you can measure in ounces (oz) and pounds (lb) if you prefer. Remember that 1,000 g = 1 kg and 16 oz = 1 lb.

# The 1-2-3 Pantry

Most of the recipes in this book are based on fresh, natural ingredients. However, a well-stocked pantry – with good olive oil in your cupboard, puff pastry in your freezer and pesto in your fridge – is essential in cooking 1-2-3.

## In the Cupboard or Pantry

Olive oil, for cooking

Extra-virgin olive oil, for salads and dressings

Vegetable oil

Cider vinegar

Balsamic vinegar

Raspberry or red wine vinegar

Light coconut milk

Condensed milk

Rolled oats

Honey

Spices: salt, pepper, cinnamon sticks, cumin, star anise, five-spice powder, black sesame or black onion seeds, white sesame seeds

Sugar: granulated, icing, dark brown, demerara (raw brown)

Nutella (chocolate hazelnut spread)

Peanut butter

Maple syrup

V8 juice

Chocolate bars and chips: milk chocolate, dark and white cooking chocolate

Unsweetened cocoa powder

Cinnamon sugar (homemade – see page 42)

## In the Freezer

Puff pastry

Vanilla ice cream

## In the Refrigerator

Pesto sauce

Mayonnaise, regular or light

Large eggs

Plain yoghurt

Parmesan cheese: use freshly grated Parmigiano-Reggiano, when possible (imported from Italy)

# Ingredients

## Substitutions

If you can't find any of the ingredients in a recipe, it is best not to make that particular recipe since I can't promise what the outcome will be! However, you generally can substitute whole milk for skimmed or semi-skimmed milk or medium eggs for large eggs with good results. The good news is that almost all of the ingredients in the recipes can be found in your local supermarket.

## Salt, Pepper and Water

These ingredients don't get counted in the three-ingredient formula because they are fundamental ingredients in cooking. So you will not find them in the ingredient lists but instead will find them in the procedures. Think of them as the free ingredients in these recipes. Water means tap water, or bottled or filtered water if you prefer. Salt generally means table salt, or pure coarse sea salt where specified. Pepper generally means black pepper that is freshly ground from a pepper mill. Sometimes white pepper is used. I have two pepper mills: one is filled with black peppercorns and one is filled with white peppercorns. In some recipes specific amounts of salt and pepper are called for; other times it says add salt and pepper to taste, which means it is up to you.

## Buying the Best

Because each recipe in this book is based on just three carefully balanced ingredients, it is important that you buy the best. Every chef knows that you can't make delicious food from inferior products. So . . . buy ingredients in season, buy the freshest-smelling and best-looking, and buy from reputable sources. If you are lucky enough to have a butcher, fish-monger, greengrocer or market that sells fresh produce, so much the better. It's fun to shop and look for the best of everything. Some-times this means paying a little more, but when you buy 'in season', fruit and vegetables are generally cheaper. Get to know the names of the people you buy from. They will love to know that you're interested in what they do.

# Equipment

You don't need to have many pots and pans to cook the recipes in this book. I use small, medium and large frying pans, or frying pans that are shallow and have slightly sloping sides. I also use a very large sauté pan with a cover. Sauté pans have straight sides and are a bit deeper than frying pans. I don't own a microwave oven or even a dishwasher. I love to wash dishes! But here's what will come in handy:

## Pots and Pans

Saucepans with lids:

approximately 2-litre (3¹/₂-pint), 3-litre (5-pint)

and 4-litre (7-pint) capacity

Very large 7-litre (12-pint) stockpot with lid

Pot fitted with a steamer basket

Wok

Small 18- and 20-cm (7- and 8-in) nonstick

frying pans

Medium-sized 22-cm (9-in) nonstick frying pan

Large 25-cm (10-in) nonstick frying pan

Very large 30-cm (12-in) nonstick sauté pan

with lid

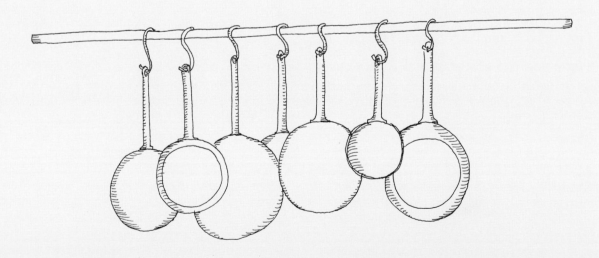

## Knives

Have a small **paring knife**. A 9-cm (3$\frac{1}{2}$-in) blade is the most common and useful. It is the 'small jobs' knife, for peeling, coring, trimming (tough outer layer of broccoli), slicing or mincing.

A **utility knife** with a 15-cm (6-in) blade is perfect for small onions and carrots, apples and pears, and the like. You also need an all-purpose 20- or 22-cm (8- or 9-in) **cook's knife** for chopping, for slicing larger fruit and vegetables, and for slicing or trimming fish and meat.

A 20-cm (8-in) **serrated knife**, with its jagged blade, is best for slicing bread, tomatoes, citrus fruits, sandwiches, brownies and cakes, and any pastry with a delicate crust.

## Electrical Applicances

I use a variety of small appliances: a blender, a food processor, and a standing mixer with a balloon whisk and paddle attachment. Or you may use a hand-held mixer. I often use my toaster, too. That's it!

## Other Things You Might Need

Baking trays

Box grater

Chopping board

Colander

Flexible rubber spatula

Garlic press

Greaseproof paper

Ice-cream maker
   (manual or electric)

Ice-cream scoop

Kitchen scales for measuring
   solid ingredients

Measuring jugs for liquids
   (usually made of glass or
   plastic)

Measuring spoons

Microplane grater

Mixing bowls

Potato masher

Vegetable peeler

Wire (mesh) sieve

Wire whisks

Wooden spoons

food processor

blender

standing mixer

'I learned that it is good to try foods you don't
know about because you might like them.'

–*Robyn Kimmel, aged 8*

# Cooking Terms

**Bake** – to cook in an oven

**Blend** – to mix foods together until they are thoroughly incorporated – no lumps!

**Boil** – to cook a liquid until large bubbles form on the surface (water boils at 100°C)

**Chop** – to use a chef's knife to cut ingredients into small pieces

**Grate** – to shred food with a box grater or with a grating blade on a food processor. When grating lemon or orange zest, it means using the smallest holes of a grater

**Grill** – to cook food underneath a source of heat, such as the grill in your oven, or to cook in a cast-iron or nonstick grill pan

**Knead** – to work dough with your hands in a folding-back and pressing-forward motion

**Preheat** – to warm up the oven before using it. This is important: preheat your oven (according to the temperature given in the recipe) at least 15 minutes before using

**Purée** – to mix in a food processor or a blender until the food is very smooth, thick, and silky – like passata

**Reduce** – to let the water in a liquid evaporate so that the resulting liquid (broth, juice, etc.) is half its original volume and is thicker and more intensely flavoured. This is done by bringing the liquid to the boil in a saucepan, lowering the heat and letting it simmer until it reaches the desired quantity

**Sauté** – to cook food in a little bit of fat (oil, butter, etc.) in a pan over high heat on the hob

**Simmer** – to cook over low heat but maintaining little bubbles

**Steam** – to put food in a steamer basket over boiling water so that the steam 'cooks' the food

**Whip** – to beat with an electric mixer or wire whisk until the ingredient (such as cream or eggs) thickens and increases in volume

**Zest** – this is the outermost coloured skin of an orange, lemon or lime. You can get long strips of zest using a vegetable peeler, or you can grate the zest on the fine holes of a box grater or microplane grater. You want to be careful not to include the white pith of the skin, which is bitter

# Hot Chocolate
# from Paris

*This recipe comes directly from my friend Dorie Greenspan, who lives in Paris for part of the year. It is especially wonderful on cold winter mornings when you're still in your pyjamas.*

**200 g (7 oz) best-quality plain cooking chocolate**
**720 ml (25 fl oz) whole milk**
**5 tablespoons sugar**

1. Chop the chocolate into small pieces and set aside.

2. In a large saucepan, put the milk, sugar and 80 ml (3 fl oz) of water. Cook over a medium heat until it begins to bubble. Remove from the heat and, using a wire whisk, whisk in the chopped chocolate. Whisk briskly until thick and smooth.

*You can serve as is, or whip up as follows:*

3. If you have a hand-held or immersion blender, use it to whip the hot chocolate for 30 seconds in the saucepan. Or, carefully transfer the mixture to a blender and whip on high speed for 30 seconds. But first you must do two things: put the top on the blender a bit askew so that hot air can escape, and cover the top with a thick towel so you don't burn your hand. **This must be done with an adult.**

*Serve while it's very hot and frothy.*

Serves 4

1.

2.

3.

Wonderful on cold winter mornings
when you're still in your pyjamas

# Tomato Sunshine

*Everyone will wonder what's in this delicious drink. Mix it up for your parents and ask them to guess! Tell them it's good for them, too.*

**240 ml (8 fl oz) V8 juice**
**240 ml (8 fl oz) orange juice**
**2 teaspoons honey**

1. Put all the ingredients in a large jar. Stir well or shake briskly.
2. Cover and chill in the refrigerator until very cold, or serve immediately over ice.

Serves 2

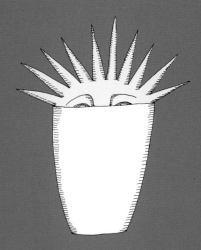

# Magic 'Coffee'

*This looks just like coffee and has a lovely sweet taste, but it uses no coffee and has no caffeine. It's magic!*

**3 tablespoons treacle**
**1 cinnamon stick**
**4 long strips of orange zest**

1. Place 720 ml (25 fl oz) of cool water in a medium-sized saucepan. Add the treacle, cinnamon stick and orange zest. Bring to the boil.
2. Lower the heat to a simmer and cook for 5 minutes, stirring occasionally.
3. Pour the liquid through a mesh strainer into 4 warm coffee cups. Garnish each with a strip of the orange zest.

*The mixture can be reheated.*

Serves 4

# Banana Frullato

*A frullato is a fresh fruit milkshake and it's a bright way to start any day.*

**1 large ripe banana**
**240 ml (8 fl oz) orange juice or pineapple juice**
**3 tablespoons condensed milk**

1. Peel the banana and cut it into 12-mm-thick (½-in) slices.
2. Put the banana slices in a blender with the juice, condensed milk and 6 ice cubes.
3. Blend on high speed until very smooth and thick.

*Serve over more ice.*

Serves 2

# Scrambled Eggs *au Fromage*

*Bonjour! Fromage means 'cheese' in French. These luscious eggs have Gruyère cheese scrambled right into them. You can substitute Emmental, but it won't have as much flavour. Serve with slices of baguette (crusty French bread) and finish with a cup of Hot Chocolate from Paris (see page 22). Bon appétit!*

**4 large eggs**
**50 g (2 oz) Gruyère cheese, in one piece**
**1 tablespoon unsalted butter**

1. Break the eggs into a medium-sized bowl.

2. Using a wire whisk or a handheld mixer, beat the eggs until thoroughly mixed and frothy.

3. Add a large pinch of salt and freshly ground black pepper.

4. Grate the cheese on the large holes of a box grater (be careful not to grate your fingers!).

5. Add ⅔ of the cheese to the eggs and mix briefly.

6. Melt the butter over a medium heat in a small (I use a 20-cm/8-in) nonstick frying pan. As soon as it melts (do not let it get brown), add the egg mixture.

7. Cook over a medium heat for about 5 minutes, stirring constantly with a wooden spoon, until thick and creamy.

8. Divide the eggs on to 2 warm plates and sprinkle with the remaining cheese.

9. Serve immediately.

Serves 2

# Omelette Crepe

*Not quite an omelette (omelettes are thick) and not quite a crepe (crepes are thin and made with flour), this is what I call an omelette crepe: an ultra-thin, tender egg preparation that gets folded in thirds and hangs over your plate. If you don't like goat cheese (but do give it a try), you can omit the cheese and place a wide ribbon of strawberry jam or Nutella (chocolate hazelnut spread) down the centre of the omelette crepe before it gets folded.*

**5 large eggs**
**100 g (4 oz) fresh goat's cheese, at room temperature**
**1½ tablespoons unsalted butter**

1. Preheat the oven to 140°C (275°F/gas mark 1).

2. Break the eggs into the bowl of an electric mixer, or use a regular bowl and a hand-held mixer. Crumble half of the goat's cheese into the bowl. Add a large pinch of salt and freshly ground black pepper. Beat until smooth.

3. Melt ¾ tablespoon of the butter in a very large nonstick sauté pan (I use a 30-cm/12-in pan). Add half of the egg mixture, making sure that it covers the bottom of pan in a very thin layer. Cook over a medium heat until the eggs begin to set but are still a little runny on top. Crumble half of the remaining cheese in a line down the centre of the eggs.

4. While they are still soft, slip a spatula under one side of the eggs and fold them over the cheese. Then fold the other side over. You will have a very long log-shaped omelette crepe about 7½ cm (3 in) wide. Cook for 1½ minutes and carefully turn the crepe over. Cook for 1 minute longer and slip on to an ovenproof plate. Put the plate in the oven to keep warm.

5. Melt the remaining butter in the pan and repeat the process with the remaining egg mixture and cheese. Serve hot.

Serves 2

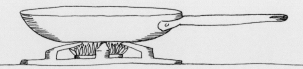

# Smiley Eggs

*Depending on the way you 'paint' your eggs, the face will look like a smiley face or the man in the moon. The 'paint' is pesto – a condiment made from fragrant basil, Parmesan cheese and pine nuts. It tastes great and can be found in most supermarkets.*

**2 large eggs**
**1 teaspoon unsalted butter**
**2 tablespoons pesto**

1. In a medium-sized bowl, beat the eggs with 1 tablespoon of water and a large pinch of salt until thoroughly mixed. If you don't mix it enough, you will have little white streaks through your egg face.

2. Melt the butter in a small nonstick frying pan (I use an 18-cm/7-in pan).

3. Pour in the beaten eggs. Let the eggs cook over a low heat for about 2 minutes until they begin to set.

4. Using a small spoon, make a smiling face: put 1 teaspoon of pesto where each eye should be and make a smile using the remaining pesto.

5. Cover the pan. Cook for 1 to 2 minutes longer until the eggs are just firm. Do not overcook. The eggs will get a little puffy and add great interest to the face.

6. Place the pan on a large heatproof plate. Smile and eat from the pan.

Serves 1

Smile and eat from the pan!

**6 fresh large eggs**

1. Put the eggs in a small, stainless-steel or enamel saucepan. Cover them with cold water.

2. Bring the water to the boil over a high heat. When the water is bubbling, and the bubbles are big, turn the heat to low. Cook the eggs uncovered at a simmer for about 10 minutes.

3. Remove the saucepan from the heat and put it into the sink. Carefully pour off the water, then run cold water over the eggs until they are cool.

4. Refrigerate the eggs for about 2 hours until very cold. (Or immediately make a Birthday Egg Cake with 1 or more eggs while they are slightly warm. See page 31.)

5. When the eggs are cold, roll them on the worktop while gently pressing on them so that the shells break up a bit. Peel them carefully, making sure to remove all the little bits of shell. Otherwise, they will *c-r-r-r-unch* in your mouth.

Makes 6

# Hard-Boiled Eggs
## and Fun Things
## to Do with Them

There are countless things you can do with a hard-boiled egg; that is, once you've learned how to make it. You can eat it as it is; you can slice it, mash it, stuff it. The egg is full of great nutrition – vitamins and minerals – and it comes apart, too. You can eat the jiggly but firm white part first, and then the yellow ball, also known as the yolk.

Eggs come in different sizes: your supermarket probably has them in medium and large, maybe extra (or very) large, too. I use extra large because my mother always did. White eggs come from hens with white feathers and white ear lobes. Brown eggs come from hens with red feathers and red ear lobes. There is no difference in taste or nutrition between white and brown eggs.

Eggs must be fresh, so check the date on the egg box. If you don't know whether an egg is fresh, put it in a bowl of cold water. If it floats to the top, don't use it! And never use an egg that has any cracks. Making a hard-boiled egg is simple if you follow a few rules.

# Black-and-White Sesame Eggs

*Hard-boiled eggs are halved and coated with tasty, crunchy seeds that make them look like little buried treasures*

**3 tablespoons white sesame seeds**
**1 tablespoon black sesame or black onion seeds**
**2 hard-boiled eggs, chilled**

1. Put the white sesame seeds in a small non-stick frying pan. Place the pan over a medium heat and toast the sesame seeds for about 1 minute until golden. Shake the frying pan back and forth to prevent sticking.

2. Remove the pan from the heat and let cool.

3. Stir in the black sesame (or black onion) seeds and ½ a teaspoon of salt.

4. Cut the eggs in half lengthwise and dip the cut halves into the seed mixture.

Serves 2

# Birthday Egg Cake

*Insert a candle and make a wish!*

**1 thick slice of brioche**
**1 warm hard-boiled egg, thinly sliced**
**1½ tablespoons light mayonnaise**

1. Trim the brioche with a small, sharp knife or cookie cutter to make a circular shape 9 cm (3½ in) in diameter. Lightly toast the bread.

2. Layer the egg slices on the toast so that they overlap slightly but lie as flat as possible.

3. Using a butter knife, spread the mayonnaise over the egg slices, adding a little on the sides, as though you were icing a birthday cake.

4. Sprinkle with salt. Eat immediately.

Serves 1

# Marble Eggs

*This is an adaptation of a Chinese recipe. After steeping in black tea for two hours, the eggs get a network of tiny, intricate lines that resemble marble. Star anise tastes like licorice but is shaped like a star, and you can find it in Asian food shops and many supermarkets. Serve with freshly cut oranges (for good luck, say the Chinese) and a stack of puffy rice cakes.*

**6 hard-boiled eggs**
**2 tablespoons loose black tea leaves**
**2 star anise, broken into pieces**

1. Tap each egg lightly on the worktop to make small cracks all over the shell.

2. Place the eggs in a medium saucepan. Add the tea, star anise and ½ a tablespoon of salt. Cover with cold water. Bring to the boil.

3. Reduce the heat to a simmer and cook, with the lid askew, for 2 hours.

4. Add more water if necessary to keep the eggs covered. Let the eggs cool in the liquid.

5. Remove the eggs and peel (discard the liquid). Serve chilled.

*You can store the eggs for up to 3 days.*

Makes 6

Real maple syrup is made from the sap of maple trees.

# Puffy Maple Pancake

*This is perfect for a weekend brunch. You will be amazed at how this maple cloud puffs up and holds its shape. The instructions say to separate the egg whites from the egg yolks. You do this by carefully cracking each egg on the side of a bowl and letting only the clear liquid dribble into the bowl. Carefully place the yolk in another bowl.*

**4 large eggs**

**6 tablespoons maple syrup**

**1 tablespoon unsalted butter**

1. Preheat the oven to 200°C (400°F/gas mark 6).

2. Separate the egg whites from the eggs yolks as described above. In the bowl of an electric mixer (or using a regular bowl and a hand-held mixer), beat together the yolks, 2 tablespoons of the maple syrup, and freshly ground black pepper for several minutes until thick.

3. Put the egg whites into another large bowl and, using clean beaters or a clean whisk, beat the whites with a ¼ teaspoon of salt until they look like thick whipped cream with firm peaks. This will take several minutes.

4. Spoon the whites into the yolks. Using a flexible rubber spatula, gently mix together until completely incorporated.

5. Melt the butter in a large ovenproof nonstick frying pan (I use a 24-cm/10-in pan) over a medium heat. Add the egg mixture to the pan and lower the heat. Cook for 2 minutes until the eggs are just set. Shake the pan to check; it should jiggle only a little.

6. Place the frying pan in the hot oven. Cook for 5 to 6 minutes until puffy and golden. Do not overcook or the pancake will collapse and be dry. Drizzle with the remaining syrup. Serve immediately.

Serves 2

# AMERICAN

## Cheesy Breakfast Polenta

*This is 'comfort food' at its best, served soft and runny or chilled and baked in squares.*

**150 g (5 oz) polenta or quick-cooking cornmeal**
**150 g (6 oz) grated mature cheddar**
**1½ tablespoons unsalted butter**

1. Put 960 ml of water plus 1 teaspoon of salt in a medium-sized saucepan. Bring to a rapid boil.

2. Lower the heat to medium-high and, using a small wire whisk, slowly add the polenta, whisking constantly until smooth. Cook for 5 minutes, stirring frequently with whisk, until thick.

3. Add 100 g (4 oz) of the cheese, butter and lots of freshly ground black pepper. Stir until smooth and cook 2 minutes longer, stirring, until very thick.

4. Serve immediately with remaining cheese scattered on top. Or, if desired, spray a 20 x 20-cm (8 x 8-in) glass baking dish with cooking spray. Pour the polenta into the dish and top with remaining cheese. Bake at 180°C (350°F/gas mark 4) for 12 minutes.

Serves 8

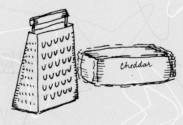

# DINER FOOD

## Lemony Potato Hash

*Use new potatoes for this unusual breakfast side dish, crispy and sun-kissed with a splash of lemon.*

**450 g (1 lb) new potatoes**
**2 tablespoons olive oil**
**1 lemon**

1. Wash the potatoes and dry well with kitchen roll. Cut the potatoes, with skin on, into 6 mm (¼ in) cubes.

2. Heat the oil in a large nonstick frying pan (I use a 30-cm/12-in pan). Add the potatoes. Cook over a high heat, stirring often, so that the potatoes do not stick. Cook until the potatoes turn golden brown.

3. After 10 minutes, add ½ a teaspoon of salt and freshly ground black pepper.

4. Continue to cook for about 6 minutes until the potatoes are tender and crispy.

5. Grate the zest of the lemon and scatter over the potatoes.

6. Cut the lemon in half and squeeze 1 teaspoon of juice over the potatoes. Cook for 1 minute longer. Serve immediately.

Serves 4

# Silver-Dollar Sausage Patties

*It is great fun to make your own sausage and you can do it in 5 minutes. Because you use turkey mince instead of pork, these are so much better (and healthier) than anything you can find in the supermarket.*

**350 g (12 oz) turkey mince**
**4 small garlic cloves**
**2 teaspoons ground cumin**

1. Place the turkey in a medium-sized bowl.

2. Peel the garlic cloves and press them (one at a time) through a garlic press.

3. Add the pressed garlic to the turkey.

4. Add the cumin, ½ a teaspoon of salt and a ¼ teaspoon of black pepper.

5. Using a fork, mash the ingredients to mix them well.

6. Cover and refrigerate for 1 hour to let the flavours mingle. Or you can cook it immediately if you're very hungry.

7. Wash your hands well. Then, using your hands, form the mixture into 12 flat patties, each about 5 cm (2 in) in diameter and 6 mm (¼ in) thick. Wash your hands well again.

8. Place a large nonstick frying pan over a medium-high heat until hot. Add the patties and cook them on one side for about 2 minutes until browned.

9. Carefully turn the patties over and cook them on the other side for about another 2 minutes until browned and cooked through. Serve immediately.

Makes 12

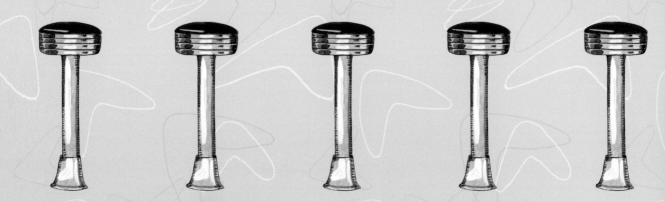

# Bacon 'Candy'

*Doesn't this sound delicious? It's great with pancakes or any kind of egg dish. The special flavour comes from five-spice powder, a Chinese seasoning made from cinnamon, cloves, coriander, ginger and black pepper. It is available in most supermarkets.*

**8 thick slices of bacon – about 225 g (8 oz)**
**1 tablespoon five-spice powder**
**2 tablespoons icing sugar**

1. Preheat the oven to 190°C (375°F/gas mark 5).

2. Carefully separate the slices of bacon.

3. In a small bowl, mix the five-spice powder and icing sugar.

4. Sprinkle each slice of bacon with the mixture to coat evenly.

5. Place the bacon slices several centimetres apart on a rimmed baking tray.

6. Bake for 15 minutes, then carefully pour off the fat (**do this with an adult**).

7. Bake for 10 minutes longer, or until crisp. Remove from the oven and let sit for 1 to 2 minutes before serving.

Makes 8 slices

Warm, comforting and delicious.
Make them for a friend!

# Warm Buttermilk Biscuits

*These flaky biscuits are sooo delicious when spread with sweet butter and topped with strawberry and orange marmalade or grape jam that you make yourself (see page 45). Have fun rolling the dough with a rolling pin and cutting out the biscuits with a cookie cutter.*

**300 g (10½ oz) self-raising flour, plus more for kneading**
**8 tablespoons unsalted butter, at room temperature**
**240 ml (8 fl oz) buttermilk, at room temperature**

1. Preheat the oven to 200°C (400°F/gas mark 6).
2. Place the flour in the bowl of a food processor. Cut the butter into small pieces and put 1 teaspoon aside for later. Put the rest of the butter into the food processor with the flour. Pulse the food processor 20 times; this means to turn it on and off very quickly to mix the butter into the flour. The flour will look crumbly.
3. Pour the flour into a bowl. Add the buttermilk and, using a wooden spoon, stir until the buttermilk is absorbed and the flour starts to pull away from the side of the bowl. This will only take a few minutes – you don't want to overdo it or the biscuits will be tough.
4. Sprinkle more flour on to a large board or on to the worktop. Put the ball of dough on the board and knead it with your hands: that means to press the dough down firmly and fold it over several times until the dough pretty much sticks together. It may look a bit lumpy, but that's OK.
5. Pat a little flour on to a rolling pin. Roll out the dough to a thickness of 12 mm (½ in). Cut out circles with a 5-cm (2-in) round cookie cutter. Using a strip of greaseproof paper, spread the remaining teaspoon of butter on a baking tray. Place the biscuits on the baking tray and bake for 20 minutes, or until the tops are golden. You may then put them under the grill for 10 seconds if you want them more golden.

Makes 14

# Petits Pains
# au Chocolate

*These small, elegant pastries are incredibly easy to prepare and will make you feel like a professional chef! Filled with oozing chocolate, they are delicious with a cold glass of milk or doubly delicious with a cup of Hot Chocolate from Paris (page 22)!*

**1 sheet frozen puff pastry – about 225 g (8 oz)**
**100-gram (4-oz) thin dark chocolate bar**
**1 egg yolk**

1. Preheat the oven to 200°C (400°F/gas mark 6).

2. Thaw the pastry at room temperature for about 30 minutes until it is bendable but still very cold. Cut the pastry sheet into 12 squares.

3. Break or cut the chocolate into 12 small rectangular pieces – about 5 cm × 2 cm (2 in × ¾ in). Place the chocolate on one edge of the pastry and roll tight, finishing with the seam on the bottom.

4. Line a baking tray with greaseproof paper. Place the rolled-up pastries, seam side down, on the paper. Press the open edges of the pastry with the prongs of a fork to seal.

5. Separate the egg. In a small bowl, whisk together the egg yolk and 1 tablespoon of water until blended. This is known as an 'egg wash'. Using a pastry brush, brush the tops of the pastry with egg wash.

6. Bake for 20 minutes, or until they are puffed and golden brown.

7. Let them cool.

Makes 12

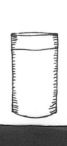

# Toasty Oats with Apple Syrup

*I never cared much for porridge when I was young, but then again, no one ever made it for me this way. Here, oats are drizzled with hot apple syrup and topped with a billow of whipped cream.*

**960 ml (33 fl oz) pure apple juice, refrigerated**
**200 g (7 oz) rolled oats**
**120 ml (4 fl oz) double cream**

1. Put 480 ml (16½ fl oz) of the apple juice in a small saucepan. Bring to the boil, lower the heat to medium and simmer for about 25 minutes until the juice is reduced by ¾. Set aside. This can be made a day ahead and reheated gently.

2. To make the porridge: in a medium-sized saucepan, pour the remaining 480 ml (16½ fl oz) of apple juice, 360 ml (12½ fl oz) water, and add a ¼ teaspoon of salt. Bring to the boil. Lower the heat to medium and add the rolled oats. Cook over a medium heat for 5 minutes, stirring frequently. Add 2 tablespoons of the double cream. Cook for 1 or 2 minutes longer until the porridge is the desired thickness.

3. Meanwhile, whip the remaining cream using a wire whisk or electric beaters. Whip just until soft peaks form. Divide the oatmeal among 4 bowls. Top with the whipped cream and drizzle with the warm apple syrup. Serve immediately.

Serves 4

## To Make Cinnamon Sugar:

*A delicious alternative to plain sugar.*

In a small bowl, stir 225 g (8 oz) sugar and 1½ tablespoons of ground cinnamon. Pour or spoon the mixture into a jar. Lasts indefinitely.

*Note: This is great for sprinkling on breakfast foods, such as cereal, toast, pancakes or porridge.*

# Dutch Breakfast

*In Holland, they serve this treat for breakfast! But it's a great snack any time.*

**1 slice of white bread**
**1 teaspoon unsalted butter, at room temperature**
**2 tablespoons chocolate sprinkles**

1. Spread the butter on the bread with a butter knife.

2. Scatter sprinkles over the bread.

Serves 1

# Sweet Almond Toast

*This is best made with challah, a braided egg bread you can buy in some bakeries and supermarkets, mainly Jewish ones. You can also use brioche or thick slices of good white bread. For a nut-free alternative, substitute cinnamon sugar for the almonds.*

**4 2-cm-thick (¾-in) slices of challah, brioche or white bread**
**4 tablespoons condensed milk**
**45 g (1½ oz) sliced almonds, with skins**

1. Preheat the oven to 190°C (375°F/gas mark 5).

2. Place the bread on a baking tray.

3. Spread 1 tablespoon of the condensed milk evenly over the surface of each slice of bread.

4. Sprinkle each slice of bread with almonds – about 2 tablespoons – to cover completely.

5. Bake for 15 to 18 minutes until the almonds are golden and the condensed milk has turned golden brown.

6. Let them cool for several minutes, but serve warm.

Makes 4

# Creamy Homemade Butter

*This is the very best butter – now say that three times quickly! – and so easy to make at home. All you need is one ingredient: double cream. You beat it and beat it and beat it and after a while the solids separate from the whey (the milky liquid), leaving you with a ball of pale yellow . . . wow . . . butter! You can make honey butter and strawberry butter, too. Or add freshly snipped chives and lime zest for a savoury butter that you can spread on corn. This recipe makes about 100 g (4 oz) of butter.*

**240 ml (8 fl oz) double cream, chilled**

1. Put the cream in the bowl of an electric mixer (or use a regular bowl and a hand-held mixer). Beat on high for 7 minutes. The cream will begin to thicken and become smooth. Then it will change suddenly and separate into small solids and a milky liquid (this is buttermilk). It will slosh around for a bit and then a few seconds later, a ball of butter will form that is separate from the milky liquid.

2. Drain off the buttermilk (you can drink it or save it for another use) and press down on the butter to release all the liquid.

3. Add a pinch of salt and stir well.

4. Put the butter in a dish. You can spread it on bread right now!

5. Or cover and refrigerate; the flavour will develop.

*Fresh butter will last up to 1 week.*

# Flavoured Butters

*To make the flavoured butters above, stir the flavouring ingredients into the butter before you refrigerate.*

### Honey Butter

**2 tablespoons honey**

**¼ teaspoon ground nutmeg**

### Strawberry Butter

**3 tablespoons strawberry jam**

**¼ teaspoon ground cinnamon**

### Chive Butter

**4 teaspoons finely chopped chives**

**½ teaspoon grated lime or lemon zest**

# Extra-Special Cream Cheeses

*These flavoured cream cheeses are great to spread on toasted bagels, muffins or pumpernickel bread.*

## Chocolate

**225 g (8 oz) cream cheese, softened**

**5½ tablespoons Nutella (chocolate hazelnut spread)**

**1 tablespoons icing sugar**

1. Put the ingredients in a medium-sized bowl.
2. Using a hand-held mixer, mix until the ingredients are well blended. Do not overmix.
3. Cover and chill.

## Maple and Raisin

**225 g (8 oz) cream cheese, softened**

**3 tablespoons maple syrup**

**50 g (1½ oz) raisins**

1. Place the ingredients in the bowl of a food processor.
2. Process briefly until all the ingredients are incorporated. Do not overprocess.
3. Cover and chill.

## Honey and Walnut

**225 g (8 oz) cream cheese, softened**

**60 g (2 oz) coarsely chopped walnuts**

**3 tablespoons honey**

1. Put the walnuts in a small nonstick frying pan.
2. Heat for 1 to 2 minutes over a medium heat, stirring often, until the nuts are toasted. Let them cool.
3. Place the cream cheese and honey in a medium-sized bowl.
4. Using a hand-held mixer, beat just until smooth.
5. Stir in the nuts.
6. Cover and chill.

## Strawberry 'Cheesecake'

**225 g (8 oz) cream cheese, softened**

**3 tablespoons strawberry jam**

**30 g (1¼ oz) icing sugar**

1. Put the ingredients in a medium-sized bowl.
2. Using a hand-held mixer, beat just until smooth.
3 Cover and chill.

## Quick Strawberry and Orange Marmalade

*Marmalade can be complicated to make and can take hours to cook, but this version is as easy and quick as can be.*

**450 g (1 lb) small ripe strawberries**

**55 g (2 oz) sugar**

**350 g (12 oz) good quality
orange marmalade**

1. Wash and dry the berries. Remove stems.

2. Cut the berries in half and place in a non-reactive (not aluminum) medium-sized saucepan.

3. Stir in sugar. Let sit for 15 minutes.

4. Cook the strawberries over a high heat for 2 minutes, stirring constantly.

5. Add the marmalade and, stirring carefully because it is very hot, cook over a high heat until the marmalade is melted.

6. Bring the mixture to the boil. Boil for 5 minutes, stirring once or twice.

7. Lower the heat to medium and cook for 15 minutes, stirring often. At this point the mixture will be bubbling away.

8. When the mixture is thick and coats the back of a wooden spoon, remove it from the heat and let it cool.

9. Transfer to a pretty bowl or jar. Cover and refrigerate until ready to use.

## The Grapiest Grape Jam

*This is the jelliest, grapiest, most delicious jam you'll ever eat!*

**480 ml (16½ fl oz) purple or
red grape juice**

**2 tablespoons honey**

**1 packet unflavoured gelatine powder**

1. Put the juice in a medium-sized saucepan.

2. Stir in the honey and bring to the boil.

3. Lower the heat to medium and sprinkle the gelatine powder over the juice. Using a small wire whisk, stir the gelatine until it dissolves. Make sure there are no lumps.

4. Continue to cook and stir for 3 minutes.

5. Remove from the heat and pour the juice into a 20 x 20-cm (8 x 8-in) square glass dish. Let it cool.

6. Refrigerate for 3 hours, or until very firm..

7. Scrape up the jam with a spoon and put into a jar. Keep refrigerated.

## Great 1-2-3 Ideas

## Two Clever Ways to Use the Chicken Wings:

1. Put the wings on a rack on a rimmed baking tray. Preheat the grill. Grill the wings for 5 minutes. Sprinkle with salt and pepper.

2. Remove the meat from the chicken wings and add to a soup or to a pasta dish.

# Heartwarming Chicken Soup

*This recipe is sooo simple and good, your mum might ask you for the recipe.*

**1 kg (2lb) chicken wings**
**4 spring onions**
**5-cm (2-in) piece of fresh ginger**

1. Each chicken wing has three sections. Cut off and discard the smallest section (called the wing tip) with a small knife. Put the wings in a 7-litre pot with a lid. Add 2.8 litres (5 pints) of cold water and 1 tablespoon of salt.

2. Thinly slice 3 of the spring onions (white and green parts) and add to the pot. Peel the ginger with a small knife, or scrape away the peel with the edge of a spoon, and slice into thin rounds. Add to the pot.

3. Bring to a full boil. Lower the heat and cover the pot. Cook over a low heat for 45 minutes; the broth should be simmering.

4. Remove the chicken wings with tongs and put them on a plate. **With the help of an adult**, strain the soup through a fine-mesh sieve set over a clean pot. Bring to the boil, lower the heat to medium, and simmer for a further 20 minutes, or until the stock is reduced to 2 litres (3½ pints). If using later, chill the stock, skim off the fat and reheat. Serve hot with the remaining spring onions, thinly sliced in soup bowls or mugs.

Serves 8

Homemade Soup—Good for when
you're on top of the world,
or feeling under the weather.

## Delicious Extras for Your Soup:

1. Spice it up with hot chilli sauce

2. Sprinkle with freshly grated Parmesan

3. Top with finely chopped chives

# Steamy Creamy Tomato Soup

*This is fresher tasting and more delicious than tomato soup that comes from a can. It uses passata, which is a thick smooth tomato sauce. For fun, you can whip a little additional double cream until thick, plop it on top of the soup and watch it melt away. Very good with Warm Buttermilk Biscuits (see page 39).*

**160 g (5½ oz) passata**
**2 tablespoons double cream**
**2 teaspoons honey**

1. Put all ingredients plus 80 ml (3 fl oz) of water in a small saucepan. Add salt and freshly ground black pepper to taste. Bring just to the boil, stirring constantly with a wooden spoon.

2. When nice and hot, pour into a mug. Let it cool a little and drink up.

*Note: You may also use a spoon.*

Serves 1

# 100-Carrot and Ginger Soup

*This soup is made with 100 baby carrots or 10 large carrots. Naturally sweet and velvety, the soup's special taste comes from fresh ginger juice that you squeeze yourself.*

**100 baby carrots or 10 large carrots – about 675 g (1½ lb)**
**10-cm (4-in) piece of fresh ginger**
**120 ml (4 fl oz) double cream**

1. If using whole carrots, trim and peel them and cut them into 2½-cm (1-in) pieces. Put the carrot pieces or baby carrots in a 4-litre saucepan with 960 ml (33 fl oz) of water and 1 teaspoon of salt. Bring to the boil, lower the heat and cover the pot. Simmer for 30 minutes, or until the carrots are very soft.

2. With a slotted spoon, transfer the carrots to the bowl of a food processor. Begin to process, slowly adding the cooking water as you go. All the water should be added.

3. Peel the ginger with a small knife, or scrape the peel away with the edge of a spoon. Grate the ginger on the large holes of a box grater. Put the grated ginger in the centre of a paper towel. Gather the corners to make a little pouch. Squeeze the ginger over a small bowl to extract the ginger juice. You will have about 1 tablespoon.

4. Add the ginger juice to the processor with 6 tablespoons of the cream. Process briefly, adding salt and pepper to taste.

5. Transfer to a saucepan and heat until hot. Pour into soup bowls and drizzle with the remaining cream.

Serves 5 to 6

## 10 Things to Do with Chicken Salad:

1. Stuff it into a scooped-out tomato shell

2. Mound it on top of a halved avocado

3. Make an open-face sandwich

4. Fill a toasted pitta pocket

5. Add diced mango and toasted almonds

6. Add chopped apples and curry powder

7. Add fresh tarragon and finely chopped red onion

8. Add diced red peppers and chopped spring onions

9. Add peas and crumbled crispy bacon

10. Spoon on to a toasted muffin; cover with cheese and grill until bubbly

# Chicken Salad 1-2-3

## How to Make It! What to Do with It!

This ancient Chinese method of cooking a whole chicken was meant to save fuel. A pot of cold water with a chicken in it is brought to the boil, and then the heat is turned off. The pot stays covered (no peeking!) until the chicken is cooked – about 3 hours. You need to listen carefully for the water to boil; it should take 20 to 25 minutes. The pot's lid will start to shake a bit and you'll hear a thump-thump – that's the water boiling. A bonus: the resulting chicken broth can be used in other recipes! Cook it until it is reduced by half.

# Chicken Salad
# 1-2-3

**1.8-kg (4-lb) chicken**
**8 tablespoons mayonnaise**
**100 g (4 oz) finely chopped celery**

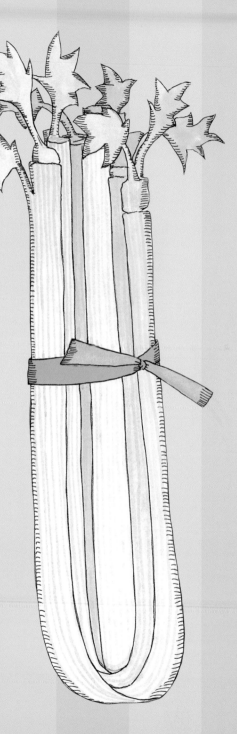

1. Wash the chicken thoroughly. If there are giblets in the cavity, discard them. Using a piece of kitchen string, tie the ends of the legs together.

2. Put the chicken in a 7-litre pot with a lid. Cover with cold water – about 4½ litres (8 pints). Add 2 tablespoons of pure coarse sea salt and 1 tablespoon of whole black peppercorns. Cover the pot. Cook over a high heat for 20 to 25 minutes until you can hear the water in the pot boiling rapidly. **Do not lift the lid.**

3. Turn off the heat. Let it sit for 3 hours. No peeking!

4. Remove the chicken from the broth. Put the chicken on a plate to cool.

5. Remove the skin and bones and cut the chicken into small pieces. Be sure to remove the meat from the wings. Put the chicken in a bowl. Discard the skin and bones.

6. In a bowl, combine the chicken with the mayonnaise and celery. Add salt and freshly ground black pepper to taste. Cover and refrigerate until ready to use.

Serves 6

# 1-2-3
# Peanut Butter

Peanut butter is the glue that holds so many great sandwiches together. Accompany any of the sandwiches on the next page with a cold glass of milk.

If you or the people you are making sandwiches for are allergic to peanuts, but not to other nuts, you may substitute almond butter or hazelnut butter for a delicious alternative. Or turn to another page for more non-nutty lunch and snack ideas!

## Make Your Own Peanut Butter

*The best food is the food you make yourself. Homemade peanut butter is clean and fresh tasting and you can control how smooth or chunky it is. Simply remove the reddish husks from shop-bought peanuts and whirl them away in your blender.*

**300 g (10 oz) unsalted roasted peanuts**
**3 tablespoons vegetable oil**
**½ tablespoon honey**

1. Remove the reddish husks from the peanuts.
2. Put half the peanuts, 1½ tablespoons of the vegetable oil, the honey and ½ a teaspoon of salt in a food processor.
3. Process until the peanut butter is rather smooth.
4. Add the remaining peanuts and oil and process again until it reaches the desired consistency. This will take about 2 minutes. (It will always look a little chunky and not like the smooth stuff you get in the supermarket.)
5. Transfer to a jar, cover and refrigerate. Keeps up to 1 week.

# Peanut Butter & Jam . . .

## Themes and Variations

### The Classic

white bread

peanut butter

jam

*(Try The Grapiest Grape Jam, page 45, or another favourite.)*

### Bananadana

cinnamon raisin bread

peanut butter

sliced bananas

### Splendido

ciabatta (Italian bread)

peanut butter

white chocolate shavings

### Country

toasted muffin

peanut butter

strawberry jam

### Frenchie

croissant

peanut butter

melted chocolate

### Dreamy

date and nut bread

peanut butter

honey

### Belgian

white bread

peanut butter

Nutella (chocolate hazelnut spread)

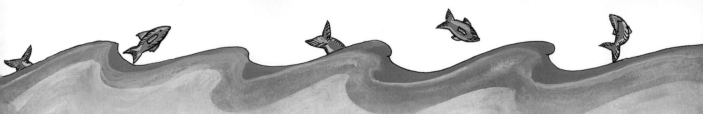

# A Tin of Tuna Fish . . .

## 1.
### Tuna Salad

**185-gram tin of tuna in oil
(about 6½ oz)**

**2½ tablespoons mayonnaise**

**2 tablespoons gherkin relish or finely
chopped gherkins**

1. Drain the tuna and put in a bowl.

2. Mix in the mayonnaise until mushy.

3. Add the relish and stir well.

4. Add a pinch of salt and pepper
   and stir again.

Makes enough for 2 sandwiches

## 2.
### Bagel Tuna Melt

**185-gram tin of tuna in water
(about 6½ oz)**

**1 large bagel (sesame is my favourite)**

**100 g (4 oz) grated mature Cheddar**

1. Preheat the oven to 200°C
   (400°F/gas mark 6).

2. Drain the tuna and put in a bowl with the
   cheese. Using a fork, mash them together
   well.

3. Add black pepper to the tuna to taste.

4. Carefully slice the bagel in half – or get an
   adult to help – and toast both pieces.

5. Pile the tuna and cheese mixture on to the
   toasted bagel halves.

6. Place on a baking tray.

7. Bake for 8 minutes. Put under the grill for 1
   minute, or until bubbly.

Serves 2

# Three Things to Do with It

## 3.

### Tuna Olive Spread

*Great for spreading on crackers or on thin white bread for tea sandwiches.*

**75 g (3 oz) cream cheese**

**185-gram tin of tuna in oil (about 6½ oz)**

**55 g (2 oz) pimento-stuffed olives, juice removed**

'The tuna olive spread was very good. I loved that. We put it in a nice little bowl and served it as a snack. Mum used it as an *hors d'oeuvres* before dinner.'

–Julia Miller, aged 11

1. Put the cream cheese in a shallow bowl and let it come to room temperature.

2. Drain most of the oil from the tin of tuna, and add the tuna to the cream cheese.

3. Mash the tuna and cream cheese together well using a fork.

4. Rinse the olives in a small strainer. Pat dry. Finely chop the olives and add to the tuna mixture. Add a little of the olive juice and salt and pepper to taste.

# Macaroni Cheese

*I invented this simple version of everyone's favourite recipe using processed cheese – the type you find inside cheeseburgers or your lunchbox. It's fun to use in cooking, too. You can use macaroni or the less familiar pasta shape called campanelle ('little bells'). If you want this even cheesier, just melt a few more slices of cheese!*

**100 g (4 oz) macaroni**
**100 g (4 oz) processed cheese slices**
**I tablespoon unsalted butter**

1. Bring a large saucepan of salted water to the boil. Add the pasta and cook for about 10 minutes until just tender.

2. Meanwhile, put 60 ml (2 fl oz) of water and the cheese in a medium-sized saucepan. Bring just to the boil. Immediately lower the heat to medium and stir with a wooden spoon for about 3 minutes until the cheese melts. Add the butter and continue to stir for 1 minute until you have a smooth sauce.

3. Put a colander in the sink and, **with the help of an adult**, drain the pasta. Return the drained pasta to the large saucepan and pour the cheese sauce over the pasta.

4. Add salt and freshly ground black pepper to taste. Stir gently while reheating the pasta.

Serves 2 or 3

# 1-2-3 Tip

*When draining the pasta, ask an adult to help you. You can skim the pasta from the water with a slotted spoon and put it in a colander, or you can pour the contents of the pot directly into a colander set in the sink. You need to be careful as the steam is very hot.*

Mac - and - cheese,
One of life's great comforts!

# Crazy Leg Drumsticks

*The nice herby taste comes from pesto – an uncooked Italian sauce made from fresh basil, garlic and pine nuts. You can find it today in any super-market. A dusting of Parmesan cheese turns into a crispy coating.*

**75 g (2½ oz) pesto**
**4 large chicken legs**
**60 g (2 oz) grated Parmesan cheeese**

1. Preheat the oven to 190°C (375°F/gas mark 5).

2. Spread pesto all over each chicken leg to cover. Sprinkle cheese all over each leg, except for the bottom where they will sit on the baking tray. You don't want the cheese to burn. Lightly press the cheese on to the chicken so it will stick. Sprinkle with freshly ground black pepper.

3 Lightly spray a rimmed baking tray with cooking spray. Place the legs on the baking tray.

4. Bake for 35 minutes until the chicken is crispy and golden.

Serves 4

# Kebabs

*In many Middle Eastern countries, minced beef or lamb is grilled on sticks or skewers. These are known as kebabs. Press the mixture with your hands on to 20-cm (8-in) wooden skewers and grill them to your liking.*

**340 g (12 oz) minced beef**
**1 small garlic clove**
**½ teaspoon ground cumin**

1. Put the minced beef in a medium-sized bowl. Peel the garlic and push it through a garlic press. Add to the beef. Add the cumin, ½ a teaspoon of salt and freshly ground black pepper and mix well.

2. Divide the mixture into 4 mounds. Using your hands, squeeze the mixture on to 4 wooden skewers, making a cylinder that is about 15 cm (6 in) long and 5 cm (2 in) wide. Flatten the mixture slightly and put the skewers on a rimmed baking tray. Cover the exposed wood of the skewers with foil so the skewers don't burn.

3. Grill under a high heat for 3 to 4 minutes until just cooked through. Do not overcook. Serve immediately.

*Note: If you don't want to grill the kebabs, you can bake them at 190°C (375°F/gas mark 5) for 8 minutes. (You don't need to cover exposed skewers with foil.)*

## Special Ingredient:
# Cumin

*Cumin is a wonderful, earthy spice that is used in many cuisines, including Mexican, Middle Eastern, Indian and Tex-Mex.*

'I must say the kebab was probably the best success we had.
It would be great for a kid that comes home in a grumpy/hungry mood. In other words, it's quick and fast to cook.'

*–Nick Green, aged 11*

*These wings fly right off the plate!*

# Sticky-Finger Wings

*You might not be able to guess what's in this Asian-tasting chicken, but you will love it anyway. The shiny brown colour and flavour comes from soy sauce and brown sugar.*

**6 very large chicken wings**
**120 ml (4 fl oz) soy sauce**
**100 g (4 oz) dark brown sugar**

1. Preheat the oven to 180°C (350°F/gas mark 4).

2. Each wing has three sections. Cut off and discard the smallest section (called the wing tip). Cut the remainder of each wing in two pieces through the joint.

3. Mix the soy sauce and sugar in a medium-sized bowl until the sugar dissolves. Add freshly ground black pepper. Add the chicken wings and mix. Marinate for 1 hour, turning the wings several times.

4. Using tongs, remove the wings from the marinade and place them on a rimmed baking tray.

5. Bake for 15 minutes. Using tongs, carefully turn the wings over. Spoon or brush a little marinade over the wings.

6. Bake for 10 minutes longer. Turn again and brush with a little marinade. The wings should be dark brown and shiny. Bake for 5 minutes longer. Serve the wings on a large plate and discard the marinade.

Serves 3 or 4

# Crunchy Fried Tomatoes

*These are a crunchy, colourful accompaniment to sandwiches and salads. Or you can eat a whole stack of them for lunch. They're also great on top of a burger!*

**4 medium-size firm tomatoes**
**150 g (5 oz) stoneground yellow cornmeal or polenta**
**vegetable oil for frying**

1. Wash the tomatoes and dry well. Slice off the top and bottom ends. Cut each tomato horizontally into 3 thick slices.

2. Place cornmeal on a flat plate. Dredge both sides of each tomato slice in cornmeal, pressing down lightly. Make sure the cut surfaces are thickly coated (sides will not get coated).

3. Heat 6 mm (¼ in) of oil in a large frying pan. When hot, carefully add the tomatoes in one layer – **you will need some adult assistance here**.

4. Cook over a medium-high heat for 2 minutes on each side, or until crispy and golden brown. Do not overcook, as you want the tomatoes to retain their shape. You may need to do this in 2 batches, adding oil as needed.

5. Drain the tomatoes on kitchen roll. Sprinkle with salt and freshly ground black pepper. Serve 3 slices per person.

Serves 4

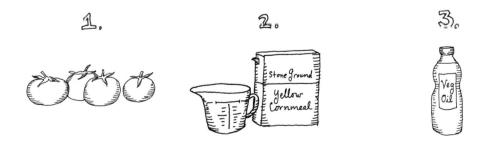

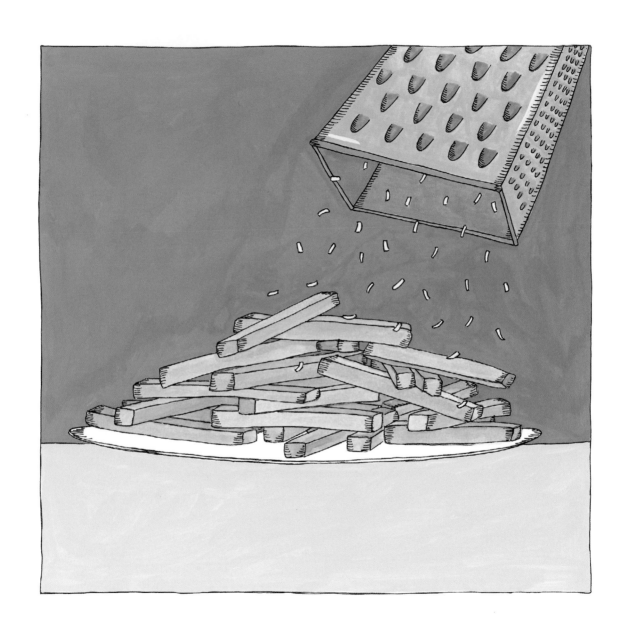

In France, chips are called 'frites'
In America, they're called 'fries'

# Parmesan Chips

*These baked chips are every bit as tasty as fried chips. They are much healthier and easier to make, too. Use baking potatoes for the best texture. Grapeseed oil helps the fries get really crispy, but you may use olive oil or vegetable oil, too.*

**3 large baking potatoes – about 750 g (1¾ lb)**
**4 tablespoons vegetable oil**
**40 g (1½ oz) freshly grated Parmesan cheese**

1. Preheat the oven to 190°C (375°F/gas mark 5).

2. Peel the potatoes. Wash them and pat dry with paper towels. Cut into chips about 7½ cm (3 in) long and 8 mm (⅓ in) wide and deep. Use a crinkle cutter if possible.

3. Place the chips in a large bowl and drizzle with 3 tablespoons of the oil. Stir until the potatoes are coated. Add ½ a teaspoon of salt and freshly ground black pepper and toss again.

4. Coat a rimmed baking tray with the remaining tablespoon of oil. Place the potatoes in a single layer on the baking tray. Bake for 20 minutes; turn the potatoes over and cook for 10 minutes. Turn again and cook for 10 minutes longer, or until the potatoes are crispy and tender.

5. Transfer the chips to a plate and sprinkle with the cheese. Serve immediately.

Serves 4

# Small Salads

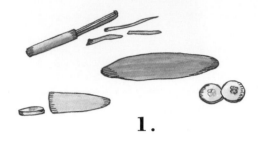

## 1.

## Cucumber Salad

**2 large cucumbers – about 550 g (1¼ lb)**

**80 ml (3 fl oz) cider vinegar**

**2 tablespoons honey**

1. Peel the cucumbers. Slice into very thin rounds. Put a colander in the sink and put the cucumbers in the colander. Sprinkle 2 tablespoons of salt over them and toss. Put a plate on top of the cucumbers and put a heavy can on the plate. This will help release the water from the cucumbers. Let sit for 30 minutes. Wash the cucumbers well under cold water to remove the salt.

2. Using your hands, squeeze the cucumbers to release the water, then put them in a bowl. Stir the cider vinegar and honey in a cup until the honey dissolves. Pour over the cucumbers and mix.

3. Add freshly ground black pepper. Cover and refrigerate until cold.

Serves 4

## 2.

## Carrot and Pineapple Salad

**4 fresh carrots – about 225 g (8 oz)**

**½ very ripe fresh pineapple or 175 g (6 oz) of canned pineapple**

**3 tablespoons mayonnaise**

1. Trim the carrots and peel them. Grate the carrots on the large holes of a box grater. Put the grated carrots in a bowl. Cut the pineapple into little cubes – about 6 mm (¼ in). You will need 175 g (6 oz). Add to the carrots along with any juice that accumulates.

2. Add the mayonnaise and stir well. Add salt and freshly ground black pepper to taste. Cover and refrigerate for several hours until cold.

Serves 4

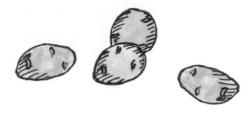

# 3.

## Potato Salad

**4 Maris Piper potatoes – about 550 g (1¼ lb)**
**1 spring onion**
**5 tablespoons mayonnaise**

1. Scrub the potatoes. Put in a large saucepan with cold water to cover by 2½ cm (1 in). Bring to the boil. Lower the heat to medium and cook for 30 minutes, or until the potatoes are just tender. To see if they're done, poke them with a skewer; if it goes in easily, go on to the next step. Carefully transfer the potatoes to a colander in the sink. Run cold water over the potatoes until they are cool enough to handle.

2. Using your fingers or a small knife, remove the skin from the potatoes and cut them into 12 mm (½ in) pieces. Place in a bowl.

3. Chop the white part of the spring onion very fine to get 1 heaped tablespoon. Add to the potatoes with the mayonnaise and 2 table-spoons of water. Stir carefully with a flexible rubber spatula.

4. Add salt and freshly ground black pepper to taste. Serve at room temperature or chilled.

Serves 4

# Savoury Breads

## Perfect Pitza

*Pizza made with pitta! Robyn Kimmel, aged 8, perfected this delicious snack and had fun testing it many times.*

**1 piece pitta bread**
**170 g (6 oz) ready-made Italian tomato sauce**
**60 g (2 oz) grated mozzarella cheese**

1. Using a small knife, cut the pitta bread open and separate it into 2 halves. If you're not very handy with a knife, just trim away the edge and pull the bread in half.
2. Toast the pitta halves until crisp and remove carefully.
3. Spread the tomato sauce evenly on the bread halves. Sprinkle with the cheese. Place under the grill for 30 seconds until golden and bubbly.

Makes 2

'Rozanne let me develop one of the recipes by myself. I made the "pizza" eight times to get it just right and so now it's called Perfect Pitza.'
–*Robyn Kimmel, aged 8*

# Avocado Mash

*My mother and I both loved this quick snack, and I was the one who made it for us when I came home from school. The secret is a very ripe avocado because it has a sweet, nutty taste.*

**½ small ripe avocado**
**1 tablespoon Italian dressing**
**1 slice white bread**

1. Scoop the avocado flesh from the hard skin. Place the avocado on a plate and mash very well with a fork. Add the dressing and mash some more.

2. Spread the avocado on the bread and sprinkle with salt and freshly ground black pepper. Cut as desired.

Serves 1

# Tomato Melt

**½ muffin**
**1 small ripe tomato**
**1 slice cheese**

1. Toast the muffin half and place it on a piece of foil.

2. Wash the tomato, pat dry and slice thinly. Place overlapping tomato slices on top of the muffin half. Sprinkle with salt and pepper. Top with the cheese.

3. Grill for 5 minutes, or until the cheese melts and gets a bit browned. Carefully remove and let it cool on a plate for 1 minute.

Serves 1

And Ian thought you could
only make popcorn in the microwave!

# Cheese Popcorn

*Ian Kimmel, aged 12, tested this recipe several times and was very excited to make popcorn on top of the hob. (He thought you could only make it in a microwave oven!) Ian especially liked shaking the pan and determining it was ready by watching the pot's lid rise a little as the popcorn peeked out.*

**3 tablespoons olive oil**
**6 tablespoons organic popcorn kernels**
**6 tablespoons grated Parmesan cheese**

1. Heat 1 tablespoon of the olive oil in a large saucepan (I use a 3-litre pan) with a lid, swirling the oil so that the bottom of the pan is coated. Add the popcorn, spreading it out to cover the bottom of the pan.

2. Cook over a medium heat until the corn begins to pop, then immediately cover the pan. Continue to shake the pan and cook for 3 minutes longer, or until all the popcorn is popped. The lid of the pan will rise a little (the popcorn and steam raise the lid).

3. Transfer the popcorn to a large bowl. While hot, add the remaining 2 tablespoons of olive oil and stir. Add the grated cheese and salt to taste. Mix well.

Serves 4

# Homemade Pretzel Sticks

*These free-form pretzel sticks are fun to make and are extra special when dipped in honey: sweet and salty at the same time!*

**I tablespoon dried yeast**
**2½ tablespoons of honey, plus 85 g (3 oz) for dipping**
**140 g (5 oz) plain flour, plus more for kneading**

1. Preheat the oven to 200°C (400°F/gas mark 6).

2. Put 120 ml (4 fl oz) of warm tap water into a large bowl. Add the yeast and 1 tablespoon of honey to the warm water, stirring until dissolved. Let sit for 8 minutes, or until yeast begins to foam.

3. Mix the flour with 1¼ teaspoons of salt and add to the yeast mixture. Stir with a long wooden spoon until a crumbly dough forms. Turn the dough out on to a worktop that has been lightly floured. Using clean hands, knead the dough for 5 minutes: using the heel of one hand, push the top part of the dough away from you. Fold that piece over and push again. Give the dough a 90° turn clockwise and repeat until the dough is smooth and no longer sticky. Divide the dough into 6 pieces and roll into long sticks, 21 cm (8½ in) long and 1¼ cm (½ in) wide. Spray a rimmed baking tray with cooking spray. Put the pretzels on the baking tray.

4. In a small bowl, mix 1½ tablespoons of the honey with 1 tablespoon of water. Using a pastry brush, brush the pretzels lightly with the honey-water mixture. Sprinkle them lightly with pure coarse sea salt. Bake for 18 to 20 minutes or until lightly browned. Let them cool. Pour 85 g (3 oz) of the honey into a small bowl. Dip the pretzels into the honey.

Makes 6

'The pretzels were very good. They were sweet and crispy. I loved kneading the bread and rolling them out. It was a lot like rolling Play-Doh.
It was a lot of fun.'

–Julia Sarah Miller, aged 11

# Carrot Sticks with Peanut Butter Dip

*Three of my young assistant chefs – Robyn, Ian and Daniel – invented this dip, which they say tastes like peanut butter cheesecake.*

**1 large carrot or 10 baby carrots**
**1½ tablespoons whipped cream cheese**
**1 tablespoon smooth peanut butter**

1. Peel the large carrot and cut into sticks, or cut the baby carrots in half lengthwise. Put on a plate.

2. In a small bowl, stir together the cream cheese, peanut butter and 1 tablespoon of water until smooth.

3. Add a pinch of salt and stir. Put in a little bowl. Use as a dip for the carrots.

Serves 1

# Cherry Tomato Skewers with Pesto Dip

*You will need 8 toothpicks.*

**8 cherry tomatoes**
**60 g (2 oz) plain yoghurt**
**1 tablespoon pesto**

1. Wash the tomatoes and dry them with a paper towel. Spear each tomato with a toothpick. Place on a plate.

2. In a small bowl mix the yoghurt and pesto thoroughly. Add salt and pepper to taste.

3. Place in a small bowl and dunk the tomatoes.

Serves 1

# Cinnamon Noodles

*Here's something different to whip up any day. It's a treat I loved as a kid. You can make your own cinnamon sugar (see page 42).*

**45 g (1½ oz) dried
wide egg noodles
1 teaspoon unsalted butter
1 teaspoon cinnamon sugar**

1. Bring a large saucepan of salted water to the boil. Add the egg noodles and cook for about 8 minutes until tender.

2. Drain the noodles well in a colander. Transfer to a flat soup bowl and toss with the butter. Add salt to taste. Sprinkle with the cinnamon sugar and serve immediately.

Serves 1

# Scrumptious Stuffed Eggs

*Make these in the morning before you leave for school. The secret here is the pickle. You may use a sweet pickle (like chutney), an Indian pickle, which is spicier and exotic (like brinjal or lime), or piccalilli, a pickle that has been mixed with mustard.*

**4 hard-boiled eggs (see page 30)
2 tablespoons light mayonnaise
3 tablespoons pickle or relish**

1. Peel the eggs and cut them in half lengthwise. Remove the yolks and place them in a bowl. Mix in the mayonnaise and mash with a fork until creamy. Add half of the relish and stir. Add salt and pepper to taste.

2. Using a spoon, fill the cavities of the egg halves with yolk mixture. Dab with a bit of remaining relish. Cover and chill until ready to serve.

Makes 8 halves

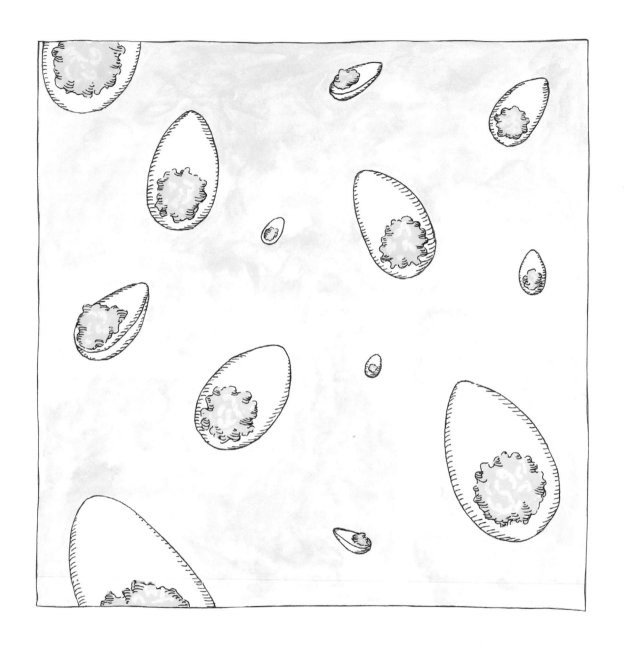

These eggs are straight
from Heaven.

# Apple Wedges with . . .

**1 medium apple *with* . . .**

**2 teaspoons peanut butter, 2 teaspoons sprinkles
(chocolate or Hundreds and Thousands)**

*or* . . .

**2 teaspoons peanut butter, 2 teaspoons maple syrup**

*or* . . .

**1 tablespoon honey, 1 tablespoon chopped
dry-roasted peanuts**

*or* . . .

**1 tablespoon honey, 15 g (½ oz) crushed pretzels**

*or* . . .

**1½ tablespoons maple syrup, 1 tablespoon toasted
sesame seeds**

1. Wash the apple and dry it well. Cut the apple into 6 or 8 wedges.
   Choose any of the options above for a healthy snack.

2. Using a butter knife, spread the peanut butter on the apple wedges
   and top with sprinkles or drizzle with maple syrup. Or drizzle
   honey or maple syrup over apple wedges and top with peanuts,
   pretzels or sesame seeds.

Serves 1

# Roasted Bananas

*When you put bananas in a hot oven, the skin turns black but the flesh becomes soft and sweet. You eat the banana with a spoon. A wonderful variation was created by Daniel Glass, aged 11 (see sidebar).*

**2 ripe medium-sized bananas in their skins**
**2 teaspoons sugar**
**2 teaspoons chocolate sprinkles**
**(sometimes called vermicelli or strands)**

1. Preheat the oven to 230°C (450°F/gas mark 8).

2. Put the bananas on a rack in the oven. Bake for 20 minutes. Remove the bananas. Carefully peel off one strip of skin on the inner curve of each hot banana. Put each banana on a plate.

3. Sprinkle each with 1 teaspoon of sugar and 1 teaspoon of chocolate sprinkles and eat with a spoon.

Serves 2

'It was so much fun to roast the bananas and eat the insides with a spoon. I invented a version of my own: place chocolate chips on the hot banana, wait one minute until the chocolate melts, and sprinkle with flaked coconut. Yum!'
        *–Daniel Glass, aged 11*

## Daniel's Variation:

1. Roast the **bananas** as directed. Place 2 teaspoons of **chocolate chips** in each hot banana. Wait for 1 minute until the chocolate melts, and sprinkle each with 2 teaspoons of flaked (sweetened) **coconut**.

# Fresh Fruit Smoothies

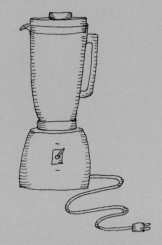

## Pineapple and Mango Smoothie

**450 g (1 lb) pineapple chunks (fresh or tinned)**
**1 ripe mango**
**480 ml (16 fl oz) vanilla soya milk, chilled**

1. Put the pineapple chunks in the freezer for several hours until hard. When ready to serve, remove the skin from the mango using a small, sharp knife. Cut away the mango flesh from the stone and cut into chunks.

4. Place the mango in a blender. Add the soya milk and frozen pineapple chunks. Process on high for 2 minutes, or longer, until very smooth. Serve immediately in tumblers or wine glasses.

Serves 4

## Blueberry and Banana Smoothie

**145 g (5 oz) fresh or frozen blueberries**
**1 very ripe banana**
**225 g (8 oz) vanilla yoghurt**

1. If using fresh berries, wash blueberries and pat dry. Put in the freezer for several hours until frozen. You can do this before you go to school.

2. Put the frozen berries in a blender. Slice the banana and add to the blender. Add the yoghurt, 8 ice cubes and 60 ml (2 fl oz) of cold water. Process on high until very smooth, thick and creamy. Add a little more water if necessary.

Serves 2

# Strawberry and Coconut Smoothie

*This is a super-duper drink! The colour looks like bubblegum and it thickens as it sits in the fridge.*

**225 g (8 oz) ripe strawberries, plus 2 extra for garnishing**
**240 ml (8 fl oz) light coconut milk**
**2½ tablespoons sugar**

1. Wash the strawberries and pat dry. Remove the stems from all but the 2 for garnishing. Cut the remaining strawberries into thick slices.

2. Put the strawberries in a blender. Add the coconut milk, sugar and 8 large ice cubes. Blend until the mixture is very smooth and thick. Serve immediately in 2 chilled glasses or refrigerate until very cold. The mixture will thicken as it sits.

3. Garnish each glass with a whole strawberry.

Serves 2

# Dinner

Dinner is easy to prepare. As a first course you can have a soup, salad or prawn cocktail, or a half-portion of pasta. Your main course should include a protein: fish, chicken, pork, lamb or beef and a side dish or two. Turn to the vegetable chapter for a rainbow of ideas including rice and grains. Keep it simple during the week and make it more elaborate at the weekend when you have more time to cook – and eat!

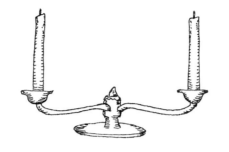

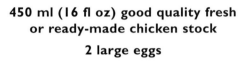

# Light-as-a-Feather Soup

*It really looks like there are lots of feathers in this bowl of soup! In Italy, it is called* stracciatella *and its third ingredient is Parmesan cheese, which gets sprinkled on top. In China, the soup is known as egg-drop soup and you add soy sauce at the end instead of the cheese. Either way, it's light as a feather.*

**450 ml (16 fl oz) good quality fresh
or ready-made chicken stock**

**2 large eggs**

**30 g (1 oz) freshly grated Parmesan
cheese or 2 teaspoons soy sauce**

1. Put the chicken stock in a small saucepan. Bring to the boil. Lower the heat to a simmer. Simmer for 5 minutes. Add a generous grinding of black pepper.

2. Break the eggs into a bowl and, using a fork, beat vigorously until well blended. Pour the beaten eggs into the soup and stir with a fork to make feathery ribbons of egg. Cook for 2 minutes until the egg is just firm. Pour the soup into 2 bowls.

3. Top with Parmesan cheese or stir in soy sauce. Serve immediately.

Serves 2

# Spinach Soup

*You can top the soup with croutons or grated cheese or a chopped hard-boiled egg.*

**2 large white potatoes – about 450 g (1 lb)**
**250 g (9 oz) fresh baby spinach, prewashed**
**5 tablespoons unsalted butter**

1. Peel the potatoes and cut into 2½-cm (1-in) chunks. Put the potatoes in a 4-litre pot with 1.8 litres (3 pints) of water and 1 teaspoon of salt. Bring to a rapid boil. Lower the heat to medium and cook for 15 minutes, or until the potatoes are becoming tender. The prongs of a fork should go in easily.

2. Add the spinach and continue to cook for 5 minutes. The potatoes will be soft and the spinach should still be bright green.

3. **Ask an adult to help you with the next step.** Using a slotted spoon, transfer the potatoes and spinach to the bowl of a food processor. Keep 450 ml (16 fl oz) of the cooking liquid. Process until the potatoes and spinach are blended. Slowly add the 450 ml (16 fl oz) of cooking liquid until smooth and thick. Slice the butter and add to the soup. Process until very smooth. Add salt and pepper to taste. Reheat before serving.

Serves 4 or more

# Mixed Green Salad with Raspberry Dressing

*You can buy your favourite pre-washed mixed green salad in any supermarket, from herb salad to baby leaf to watercress, spinach and rocket. Balsamic vinegar can be used instead of raspberry.*

**1 tablespoon raspberry vinegar**
**60 ml (2 fl oz) olive oil**
**100 g (4 oz) mixed greens, chilled**

1.  Pour the raspberry vinegar into a cup. Using a fork, slowly whisk in the olive oil until well blended. The dressing will 'emulsify' or thicken.

2.  Wash the greens, if necessary, and dry well using paper towels or a salad spinner, which is a lot of fun to use. Put the greens in a large bowl. Pour the dressing over them and toss well. Add salt and freshly ground black pepper to taste. Serve immediately.

Serves 4

## Great 1-2-3 Idea

## Quick Salad Dressing

*Here's a great dressing you can make in a snap. You can buy American yellow mustard in most supermarkets now — it's very mild. Or you can use Dijon mustard, which is French, but a bit hotter so you may want to use less of it!*

**80 g (3 oz) ketchup**

**2 tablespoons American yellow mustard**

**1½ tablespoons honey**

Mix in a small bowl until well blended.

# Iceberg Salad with Blue Cheese and Bacon

*Fun iceberg lettuce tip: slam the bottom of the head on a wooden board and the core will simply fall out! Or ask an adult for some help.*

**175 g (6 oz) mild blue cheese**
**8 slices bacon**
**1 large head of iceberg lettuce**

1. Crumble the cheese into small pieces. Put 130 g (4½ oz) of the cheese in the bowl of a food processor. Process the cheese while you slowly add 120 ml (4 fl oz) of cold water, a little at a time. Blend until completely smooth. Transfer to a bowl. The dressing will thicken as it sits. Cover and refrigerate until cold. Add a little water if the dressing is too thick.

2. Cook the bacon in a large nonstick frying pan on a medium heat until just crispy. Transfer on to paper towels to drain.

3. Cut the lettuce into 6 wedges. Put 1 wedge on each of 6 plates. Spoon the dressing over the lettuce and crumble the bacon on top. Sprinkle with a little of the remaining crumbled cheese.

Serves 6

# Bowties with Broccoli

*This is a two-in-one recipe because the broccoli florets are tossed with the pasta while the broccoli stems become a buttery sauce! I like to use bowtie-shaped pasta (known as* farfalle *in Italian). But there are hundreds of shapes to choose from.*

**1 very large head of broccoli**
**3 tablespoons unsalted butter, chilled**
**225 g (8 oz) bowtie pasta**

1. Cut off all the florets from the head of broccoli, leaving their stems 12 mm (½ in) long. Cut these pieces in half lengthwise and set aside.

2. Using a vegetable peeler, peel the long stems and discard the peelings. Cut the stems into 2½-cm (1-in) pieces. Put the stems in a small saucepan with 280 ml (10 fl oz) of water. Bring to the boil. Lower the heat to a simmer, cover the pot and cook for about 15 minutes until the broccoli is very soft. Let it cool for 5 minutes.

3. **With the help of an adult**, transfer the cooked broccoli stems and cooking liquid to a blender. Process until smooth. Add small knobs of butter and process again until very smooth and creamy. Add a little water if the sauce is too thick. Add salt and pepper to taste. Transfer the sauce to a small saucepan and reheat when the pasta is almost cooked (see next step).

4. Meanwhile, bring a large pot of salted water to the boil. Add the pasta and cook for 8 minutes. Add the halved broccoli florets and cook for 5 minutes longer, or until the pasta and broccoli are tender. Do not overcook; you want the broccoli to be bright green. Drain well in a colander. Divide the pasta with broccoli among 4 bowls. Pour the hot sauce over the top and serve immediately.
*Optional: top with a curl of chilled butter before serving.*

Serves 4

You can wear a bowtie to dinner,
or you can eat a plate of them.

# White-and-Green Pasta in Tomato Sauce

*Tagliatelle that comes packaged with both white and green noodles looks great tossed in tomato sauce. There are lots of different tomato sauces available; you can use one flavoured with roasted garlic or herbs, if you wish.*

**225 g (8 oz) white-and-green tagliatelle or fettuccine**
**240 g (8½ oz) passata (smooth tomato sauce)**
**160 ml (5½ fl oz) single cream**

1. Bring a large pot of salted water to the boil. Add the pasta and cook for 10 to 12 minutes, or until the pasta is tender. Do not overcook as you don't want the pasta to be mushy.

2. Meanwhile, pour the tomato sauce and cream into a small saucepan. Cook over a medium-high heat, whisking with a wire whisk until smooth and hot. Add salt to taste.

3. When the pasta is done, drain in a colander set in the sink. Shake off all the water and transfer the pasta to 4 warm bowls. Spoon hot sauce over the pasta and serve immediately with a sprinkling of freshly ground pepper.

Serves 4

# Pineapple-Glazed
# Salmon Steaks

*Salmon steaks are cut across the width of the fish into portions with a small bone in the centre. Pineapple juice and soy sauce make a magical glaze.*

**480 ml (16 fl oz) unsweetened pineapple juice**
**4 teaspoons soy sauce**
**4 175-g (6-oz) salmon steaks**

1. Put the pineapple juice in a small saucepan. (Do not use aluminum because it will create an undesirable chemical reaction.) Bring to the boil. Lower the heat to medium and cook until the juice is reduced by half. Remove from the heat and cool. Stir in the soy sauce.

2. Place the salmon in a shallow casserole dish. Pour the pineapple and soy mixture over the fish. Add a grinding of black pepper. Refrigerate for 2 hours, turning the fish after the first hour.

3. Place a very large nonstick sauté pan (I use a 30-cm/12-in pan) over a medium heat until hot. Add the salmon and cook for 3 minutes. Using a spatula, carefully turn the fish over and cook for 3 to 4 minutes until just cooked through. Do not overcook.

4. Meanwhile, put the remaining pineapple and soy mixture into a small frying pan. Cook over a high heat for about 5 minutes until reduced by half. Using a pastry brush, brush the top of the salmon with some of the reduced marinade. Remove the fish from the pan and serve.

Serves 4

# Prawn Cocktail
# with Seafood Sorbet

*It is great fun to dunk the cooked prawns into the slushy cocktail 'sorbet'.*

**240 ml (8 fl oz) seafood sauce**
**3 lemons**
**450 g (1 lb) very large prawns (in their shells)**

1. Put the seafood sauce into a small bowl. Using the fine holes of a box grater, grate the zest of the lemon. Be careful not to get any of the bitter white pith. Add the grated rind zest to the seafood sauce. Squeeze the lemon to get 2 tablespoons of juice. Add to the bowl and stir. Place the bowl in the freezer and stir every 30 minutes for about 2 hours until a firm but slushy texture forms.

2. Wash the prawns in cold water. Bring a medium-sized saucepan of water to a rapid boil. Add 80 g (3 oz) of pure coarse sea salt or more – so that it tastes as salty as the sea. Add the prawns and lower the heat to medium. Cook for 3 to 4 minutes until the prawns are just pink and firm. Drain the prawns and put them in a bowl of heavily salted ice-cold water for 10 minutes.

3. Peel the prawns, leaving the tails intact. Cut the remaining lemons in half across the width to get 4 halves. Slice 6 mm (¼ in) or so from the bottom of each half so that it sits upright without wobbling. Scoop out the flesh and discard. Using a small ice-cream scoop, put seafood 'sorbet' into each lemon cup, mounding it up high. Put one in the centre of each of 4 plates. Surround with prawns and serve immediately.

Serves 4

# Fillet of Sole
# with Lemon Butter

*You can use fillets of flounder instead of sole, and fresh lime instead of lemon!*

**4 175-g (6-oz) sole fillets, skin removed**
**6 tablespoons (75 g/3 oz) unsalted butter, chilled**
**2 large lemons**

1. Season the fish with salt and pepper. Melt 3 tablespoons of the butter in a very large nonstick frying pan. Cook the fish over a high heat for about 3 minutes on each side until golden and slightly crispy. Then transfer the fish, using a spatula, to a warm plate. Cover with foil.

2. Add the juice of 1 lemon to the pan and let the sauce bubble up. Cook until the butter is nut-coloured, or light brown: be careful not to burn it. Remove from the heat and add the remaining 3 tablespoons of chilled butter. Swirl the pan until the butter melts. Heat briefly, adding salt and pepper to taste. Pour the sauce over the fish. Top with very thin slices of the remaining lemon, if desired.

Serves 4

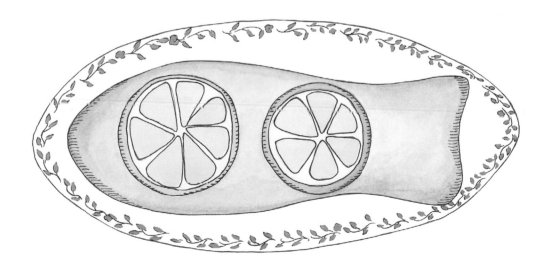

## Quick 1-2-3 Gravy

1. To make a quick gravy, pour 240 ml (8 fl oz) of water into the roasting pan and scrape up the browned bits.

2. Pour through a fine strainer into a small saucepan.

3. Bring to the boil and cook over a high heat until the juices thicken.

4. If using butter, add a tablespoon of cold butter to enrich the sauce. You can add some finely chopped thyme or a squeeze of the cooked lemon to the sauce.

# Simple Roast Chicken

*Every meat-eating kid should know how to roast a chicken. Flavour it with fresh thyme or lemon. Baste it with melted butter or olive oil. Delicious every way.*

**1.8-kg (4-lb) roasting chicken**

**1 bunch of fresh thyme or a lemon, pierced several times with a fork**

**4 tablespoons melted butter or olive oil**

1. Preheat the oven to 180°C (350°F/gas mark 4).

2. If the chicken comes with giblets, you need to remove these from the cavity of the chicken and discard. Wash the chicken and dry well.

3. Fill the cavity with the fresh thyme or the lemon. With kitchen string, tie the legs together. Tuck the wings under the chicken. Put the chicken on a rack on a rimmed baking tray. Rub salt all over the chicken. Drizzle with half of the melted butter or olive oil.

4. Roast for about 1 hour and 40 minutes, basting several times during roasting with the remaining butter or oil.

5. When the chicken is done, remove it from the oven. Transfer the chicken to a platter and sprinkle with salt and freshly ground black pepper. Remove the thyme or lemon. Carve the chicken as desired, asking an adult to help.

*Serves 6*

'A simple roast chicken is something every kid should know how to make.
You can do it your way. With olive oil or butter, and then flavour it with
fresh thyme, lemon, or garlic. Using butter and garlic is my favourite way.'

–Danielle Hartog, aged 11

# Ketchup and Cola Chicken

*Finger-licking good, this is great hot, cold or in between. You can substitute root beer for the cola if you like.*

**240 g (8½ oz) ketchup**
**240 ml (8 fl oz) Pepsi, Coke or other cola**
**1½-kg (3½-lb) chicken, quartered**

1. Preheat the oven to 180°C (350°F/gas mark 4).

2. In a large bowl, whisk together the ketchup and cola until thoroughly mixed. Wash the chicken and pat dry with paper towels. Remove the wings from the chicken breast quarters. Put all of the chicken pieces in the bowl and toss so that the chicken is coated with the ketchup and cola mixture. Leave for 30 minutes or, refrigerated, up to 8 hours.

3. Remove the chicken, reserving the marinade. Place the chicken, skin side up, on a rimmed baking tray. Sprinkle the chicken with salt and freshly ground black pepper. Bake for 1 hour. Meanwhile, put the marinade in a small saucepan and bring to the boil. Reduce the heat to medium and cook for about 15 minutes until the marinade is reduced to 240 ml (8 fl oz). During baking, baste the chicken with the reduced marinade several times, using a pastry brush. After 30 minutes, **ask an adult to help you** transfer the chicken to a plate, pour off the fat and return the chicken to the pan. Continue cooking for 30 minutes.

4. When the chicken is done, transfer it to a warm plate. Drizzle with a little more warm marinade, serving any extra on the side.

Serves 4

# Three-Minute Chicken

*This looks like a big open-face melted ham-and-cheese sand-wich. But instead of the bread there's a nice fillet of chicken breast! You assemble it in 3 minutes; then bake it for 7.*

**4 150-g (5-oz) chicken breasts**
**4 slices of ham, 20 g (¾ oz) each**
**4 slices of Emmental cheese, 25 g (1 oz) each**

1. Preheat the oven to 190°C (375°F/gas mark 5).

2. Spray a rimmed baking tray with cooking spray or line with foil. Sprinkle lightly with salt and pepper.

3. Place the chicken breasts on a baking tray, well spaced apart. Place a piece of ham on each piece of chicken. Place a slice of cheese on the ham. Bake for 7 minutes, or until the cheese is melted (but not running all over the baking tray!) and the chicken is cooked through – no pink! Do not overcook. Serve immediately with a colourful side dish.

Serves 4

*Note: If your chicken breasts are very bulky and weigh more than 150 g (5 oz), you can carefully cut them in half as though you were slicing a bread roll. Ask an adult to help you.*

# Rosemary Meatballs

*It's amazing how moist low-fat turkey can taste, provided you don't overcook the meatballs. All my young friends love them.*

**225 g (8 oz) lean turkey mince**
**I small onion**
**2 branches of fresh rosemary**

1. Put the turkey in a medium-sized bowl. Peel the onion and cut it in half. Grate the onion on the large holes of a box grater to get 2 tablespoons of grated onion juice and pulp. Add to the turkey.

2. Remove the leaves from I rosemary branch and chop as fine as possible to get I teaspoon of chopped rosemary. Add a little less than ½ a teaspoon of salt and a ¼ teaspoon of freshly ground black pepper. Mix until all the ingredients are blended. Form the mixture into 16 balls.

3. Heat a large nonstick frying pan until hot. Add the meatballs and cook for 2 minutes over a high heat; lower the heat to medium and roll the meatballs around the pan so they don't stick. Cook for 3 to 4 minutes longer until just firm. Do not overcook. Serve immediately, garnished with fresh rosemary sprigs.

Makes 16 (serves 2 or 3)

# Chicken Ooh-la-la

*Boursin cheese, imported from France, is something I've loved since I was a kid. It's flavoured with herbs and garlic and is smooth and creamy. You can substitute fresh herbed goat's cheese. Make this recipe with a crust of finely chopped pecans or a sheer layer of orange marmalade. Either way it's ooh-la-la.*

**150 g (5 oz) Boursin cheese**
**4 large skinless, boneless chicken breasts**
**90 g (3 oz) chopped pecans or 4 tablespoons orange marmalade**

1. Let the cheese come to room temperature. Preheat the oven to 180°C (350°F/gas mark 4).

2. Using a butter knife, spread the cheese on each breast to completely cover.

3. If using pecans, chop them very fine. Sprinkle 3 tablespoons of pecans evenly over each breast and pat in lightly. Or, using a butter knife, spread 1 tablespoon of marmalade on each breast to coat cheese lightly and evenly.

4. Spray a rimmed baking tray with cooking spray or line with foil. Put the chicken breasts on a baking tray well spaced apart. Bake for 25 minutes. Do not overcook. Serve immediately.

Serves 4

**Great 1-2-3 Idea**

## To Make Spring Onion Brushes:

1. Remove the dark green parts from 8 spring onions, leaving only 5 cm (2 in) of the light green part.

2. Cut off the root ends to make them even.

3. Make 5-cm (2-in) slits up the white part of the spring onion, as if cutting them into quarters, leaving 2½ cm (1 in) uncut at the light green top.

4. Put them in a deep bowl of cold water.

5. Cover and refrigerate for 2 hours, or until the spring onions curl up into little brushes.

Makes 8

# Yummy Meatballs

*These are very easy to make. And you garnish them with cool-looking spring onion 'brushes'. Instead of making meatballs, you can form the mixture into 4 big oval 'chopped steaks' and grill them.*

**2 bunches of spring onions**
**680 g (1½ lb) beef mince**
**3 tablespoons teriyaki sauce**

1. Wash the spring onions. Cut off the dark green parts from the spring onions and discard. Chop enough of the white parts of the spring onions to get 25 g (1 oz) finely chopped.

2. Place the meat in a large bowl. Add the spring onions, 2 tablespoons of the teriyaki sauce, ½ a teaspoon of salt and freshly ground black pepper. Using clean hands, combine the ingredients thoroughly. Form into 24 meatballs that are about 4 cm (1½ in) in diameter.

3. Heat a very large nonstick sauté pan (I use a 30-cm/12-in pan) until hot. Add the meatballs and cook over a high heat for about 10 minutes, rolling the meatballs around so they brown and become a little crispy on all sides. Using a slotted spoon, place the meatballs on a serving dish and sprinkle with the remaining teriyaki sauce.

Makes 24

Throw a party and serve
these festive meatballs!

# Pork Chops
# with Sautéed Apples

*This is an adaptation of a simple French recipe that any kid can make. Braeburn apples sautéed in butter taste better than pie. Rib chops, not loin chops, are best for this dish.*

**2 thick pork chops – about 200 g (7 oz) each**
**1 large Braeburn apple**
**2 tablespoons unsalted butter**

1. Season the pork chops with salt and freshly ground black pepper.

2. Peel the apple. Cut the apple in half. Cut each half into 5 wedges. Remove the seeds.

3. Melt the butter in a 25-cm (10-in) frying pan. Add the apples and cook over a medium-high heat for 1 minute on each side. Add the pork chops and cook for 4 minutes. Turn the pork chops and apple wedges over. The butter will turn brown (do not let it turn black): this is known as brown butter or *beurre noisette* in French. Cook for 3 to 4 minutes longer until just firm. Do not overcook or the pork will get dry.

4. Remove the pork chops and apples from the pan. Serve immediately.

Serves 2

# Juicy Pork with Prunes

*In case you were wondering, prunes are dried plums. This is a beautiful and delicious dish to share with friends. Make sure the cheese is finely grated.*

**400-g (14-oz) pork fillet**
**10 small pitted prunes**
**40 g (1½ oz) freshly grated Parmesan cheese**

1. Preheat the oven to 190°C (375°F/gas mark 5).

2. Cut a 2½-cm (1-in) deep slit down the entire length of the fillet, leaving 2½ cm (1 in) on each end uncut. The idea is to make a deep channel in the pork fillet so that you can stuff it with prunes.

3. Place the prunes side by side in the channel and sprinkle with all but 1 tablespoon of the cheese. Cut 8 15-cm (6-in) pieces of string. Tie the fillet at 4-cm (1½-in) intervals, pulling tight so that the prunes are covered. Season the pork with salt and freshly ground black pepper.

4. Spray a rimmed baking tray with cooking spray. Put the fillet on the baking tray and dust with the remaining cheese. Bake for 20 minutes. Remove from the oven. Let the pork rest for 5 minutes. Cut into 12-mm (½-in) thick slices and serve immediately.

Serves 4

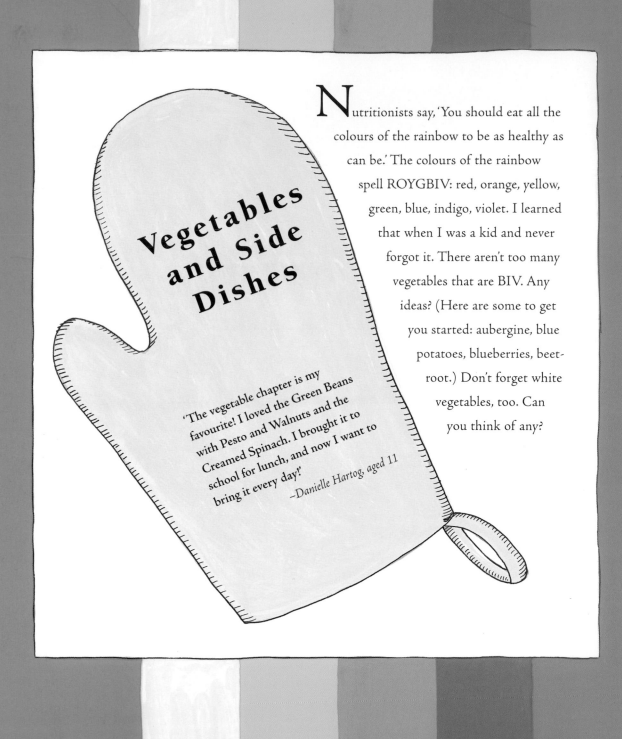

# Vegetables and Side Dishes

'The vegetable chapter is my favourite! I loved the Green Beans with Pesto and Walnuts and the Creamed Spinach. I brought it to school for lunch, and now I want to bring it every day.'

–Danielle Hartog, aged 11

Nutritionists say, 'You should eat all the colours of the rainbow to be as healthy as can be.' The colours of the rainbow spell ROYGBIV: red, orange, yellow, green, blue, indigo, violet. I learned that when I was a kid and never forgot it. There aren't too many vegetables that are BIV. Any ideas? (Here are some to get you started: aubergine, blue potatoes, blueberries, beetroot.) Don't forget white vegetables, too. Can you think of any?

# Carrots
## Three Ways

### *Simple*

#### Glazed Carrot Coins

*This technique produces a lovely glaze for the carrots. Instead of parsley, you might use a sprinkling of grated lemon zest or nutmeg.*

**450 g (1 lb) carrots**
**1½ tablespoons butter**
**3 tablespoons chopped flat-leaf parsley**

1. Peel the carrots and cut them into thin round slices – about 3 mm (⅛ in) thick. Put them in a 3-litre saucepan. Add 240 ml (8 fl oz) of water and a ¼ teaspoon of salt. Slice the butter and scatter on top. Bring to the boil. Cover the pan and reduce the heat to medium-high. Cook for 10 minutes and then uncover the pan. Cook for a few minutes longer until the carrots are tender.

2. Using a slotted spoon, transfer the carrots to a heatproof bowl. Reduce the liquid in the pan until it is thick and syrupy, and pour it over the carrots. Toss with salt and freshly ground black pepper. Sprinkle with the parsley.

Serves 4

# Fun

## Carrot Fries
## with Mint

*With a simple kitchen tool that cuts potatoes
into crinkly French fries, you can cut carrots into
similar shapes. Or cut them with a knife with the
help of an adult. Fresh basil may be substituted
for the mint.*

**450 g (1 lb) long slender carrots**
**3 tablespoons olive oil**
**1 bunch of fresh mint**

1. Preheat the oven to 190°C (375°F/gas mark 5).

2. Peel the carrots. Using a crinkle cutter or a
   large knife, cut the carrots in half across the
   width. Cut the slender half lengthwise into
   2 long pieces. Cut the thicker half lengthwise into 4 long pieces: the goal is to get
   carrot sticks shaped like French fries.

3. Put the carrots on a rimmed baking tray.
   Drizzle with the oil. Using clean hands, toss
   the carrots so that they are completely
   coated with oil. Sprinkle with salt and freshly
   ground black pepper. Roast for 20–25 minutes until tender, turning the carrots once
   or twice during baking. The carrots will be
   golden brown. Transfer to a serving dish.

4. Wash the mint (or basil) and dry well. Cut
   into very thin strips to get 2 tablespoons.
   Scatter over the carrots.

Serves 4

# Divine

## Baby Carrots
## with Sweet Garlic

*You will be surprised how sweet the garlic
becomes when it is cooked long and s-l-o-w-l-y.*

**450 g (1 lb) baby carrots**
**10 garlic cloves**
**3 tablespoons olive oil**

1. Place the carrots in a 4-litre saucepan.

2. Peel the garlic and cut in half lengthwise.
   Add to the carrots. Add the olive oil and
   160 ml (5½ fl oz) of water. Add ½ a teaspoon of salt and bring to the boil. Reduce
   the heat to very low and cover the pan.
   Simmer for 30 minutes, or until the carrots
   are tender, stirring several times during
   cooking.

3. With a slotted spoon, transfer the carrots
   and garlic to a bowl. Cook the pan juices
   over a high heat for about 5 minutes until
   thick and syrupy. Toss with the carrots,
   adding salt and freshly ground black pepper
   to taste.

Serves 4

# Corn-on-the-Cob with Honey Butter

*Few vegetables are more fun to eat than corn-on-the cob, especially when it's slathered with sweet honey butter that drips down your chin! Break the cobs in half with your hands to make 'mini corns'.*

**4 tablespoons (55 g/2 oz) unsalted butter at
room temperature
1 tablespoon honey
2 large sweetcorn cobs**

1. Put the butter in the bowl of an electric mixer or simply put it in a bowl. Add the honey and a pinch of salt. Beat with the electric mixer until smooth and creamy, or mash the butter and honey together until thoroughly blended. Set aside.

2. If necessary, remove the husk (that's the green outer leaves) and silk (those are the long, golden threads under the husk) from the corn. Place both hands firmly on each cob and break in half, as evenly as possible, to get 2 smaller pieces. You may need an adult to help you.

3. Bring a medium-sized saucepan of water to the boil. Add the corn and lower the heat to medium. Cover the saucepan and cook the corn for about 8 minutes.

4. Using tongs, transfer the corn to a dish. Sprinkle lightly with salt. Top with the honey butter and serve immediately.

Serves 4

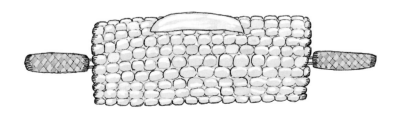

# Cauliflower Popcorn

*Roasting small cauliflower florets turns them into yielding, golden nuggets that become addictive when topped with sharp Cheddar.*

**1 large head of cauliflower**
**3 tablespoons extra-virgin olive oil**
**100 g (4 oz) grated mature white Cheddar cheese**

1. Preheat the oven to 200°C (400°F/gas mark 6).

2. Cut the cauliflower in half. Remove the core with a small knife and discard. Break the head into small florets – about 2-cm (¾-in) pieces. Place in a bowl. Toss with the olive oil and sprinkle with salt and pepper. Place on a rimmed baking tray and roast for 35 to 40 minutes until soft and caramelised (they will turn golden brown), turning once during cooking. Shake the pan several times during baking so that the cauliflower doesn't stick. **Ask an adult to help you with this.**

3. Transfer the cooked cauliflower to a serving dish. Add salt and freshly ground black pepper and sprinkle with the cheese. Serve hot or at room temperature.

Serves 4

# Cauliflower with Garlicky Breadcrumbs

1. Break **1 large head of cauliflower** into large florets. Boil in salted water for 15 minutes, or until tender. Drain well in a colander.

2. Meanwhile, put **1 tablespoon of garlic oil** in a small frying pan. Add **30 g (1 oz) seasoned breadcrumbs**. Cook for several minutes, stirring constantly, until the crumbs are crispy. Add salt and freshly ground black pepper to taste.

3. Drizzle several table-spoons of garlic oil over the hot cauli-flower and scatter the breadcrumbs on top.

Serves 4

# Chinese-style

## Asparagus-in-a-Wok

*It is best to use slender asparagus. This way the dish can be stir-fried in less than 5 minutes.*

**570 g (1¼ lb) slender asparagus**
**I large red, yellow or orange pepper**
**I tablespoon garlic oil**
**(or extra-virgin olive oil)**

1. Remove the woody bottoms of the asparagus, then trim the stalks to equal length. Cut each asparagus stalk on the bias into 5-cm (2-in) pieces. ('On the bias' means that instead of cutting straight across each stalk, you cut at an angle.)

2. Cut off the panels (the 4 sides) of the pepper to get 4 rectangular shapes. Remove the seeds, then cut the panels into strips that are about 5 cm (2 in) long and 3 mm (⅛ in) wide.

3. Heat the oil in a wok or large sauté pan. Add the asparagus and pepper strips. Stir-fry over a medium-high heat for about 3 minutes, tossing constantly, until the asparagus begins to brown. Add 1 tablespoon of water and continue to cook, stirring constantly, until tender but still a little crunchy. Toss with salt and freshly ground black pepper.

Serves 4

## Steamed Broccoli with Stir-Fried Pecans

*You can cut the florets from a large head of broccoli or simply buy 450 g (1 lb) of florets. This is the best way imaginable to get anyone to eat broccoli, but don't reveal the secret ingredient until you get compliments.*

**I large bunch of broccoli**
**60 g (2 oz) coarsely chopped pecans**
**3 tablespoons teriyaki sauce**

1. Cut the broccoli into large florets, leaving 4 cm (1½ in) of the stem attached. (You will have about 450 g/1 lb florets.) Place the broccoli in a steamer basket and steam, covered, over boiling water for about 8 minutes until soft but still bright green.

2. Meanwhile, toast the pecans in a small non-stick frying pan over a medium heat. Stir them constantly until toasted (dark brown), being careful not to let them burn.

3. In a large bowl, toss the hot broccoli with the toasted pecans and teriyaki sauce. Season with salt and freshly ground black pepper. Serve immediately.

Serves 4

# Chinese-style

## Mangetout and Baby Corn

*I loved to eat miniature baby corn as a kid. It is available fresh or frozen in most supermarkets and is delicious and colourful paired with crunchy mangetout. Mangetout is a type of pea that grows in a long flat pod. You eat the whole pod.*

**450 g (1 lb) fresh mangetout**

**425 g (15 oz) whole baby corn**

**1½ tablespoons sesame oil**

1. Wash the mangetout. Pat dry. Trim the ends and remove the strings running along the side.

2. Place the corn in a colander and wash under cold water. Pat dry.

3. Put the mangetout and corn in a steamer basket and carefully set the basket over a pot of boiling water. Cover and cook for 8 minutes, or until the mangetout are tender but still bright green.

4. Transfer the vegetables to a bowl and toss with the peanut or sesame oil. Add salt and freshly ground black pepper to taste.

Serves 4

'I made the mangetout and baby corn totally on my own. The sesame oil gave the vegetables a really yummy taste. My little sister loved the corn and so did I.'

–Danielle Hartog, aged 11

# Broccoli Spears with Cheese Sauce

*This sauce is sooo easy to make and it looks just like a classic French cream sauce known as* Mornay. *The cheese should be grated on the small holes of your grater, so that it looks like sand.*

**2 thick broccoli spears – about ½ head**
**80 ml (2¾ fl oz) milk**
**60 g (2 oz) grated Parmesan cheeese**

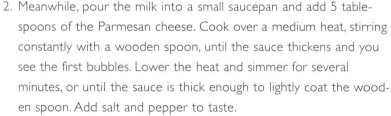

1. Place the broccoli spears in a saucepan large enough to hold them without overlapping. Cover with enough water to come almost to the top of the broccoli. Add ½ a teaspoon of salt and bring to a full boil. Cover the saucepan and lower the heat to medium-high. Cook for 12 minutes or until tender, but do not overcook. The broccoli should still be bright green.

2. Meanwhile, pour the milk into a small saucepan and add 5 table-spoons of the Parmesan cheese. Cook over a medium heat, stirring constantly with a wooden spoon, until the sauce thickens and you see the first bubbles. Lower the heat and simmer for several minutes, or until the sauce is thick enough to lightly coat the wooden spoon. Add salt and pepper to taste.

3. Drain the broccoli well and place on a serving dish. Pour the hot cheese sauce over the broccoli and sprinkle with the remaining grated cheese and freshly ground black pepper.

Serves 2

# Creamed Spinach

*There is no cream in this dish; instead the wonderfully creamy texture comes from puréed cottage cheese. No one will know! Frozen spinach works especially well in this recipe.*

**2 packs frozen leaf spinach – about 285 g (10 oz) each**
**285 g (10 oz) low-fat cottage cheese**
**2½ tablespoons unsalted butter**

1. In a large saucepan with a lid, combine 120 ml (4 fl oz) of water and ½ a teaspoon of salt and bring to the boil. Add the frozen spinach and bring to the boil. Cover and reduce the heat to medium-high. Cook for 10 minutes, stirring several times. The spinach should still be bright green. Drain thoroughly in a colander set in the sink. Make sure to shake out all the water. Pat the spinach dry with paper towels.

2. Transfer the hot spinach to a food processor. Add the cottage cheese and all but 1 teaspoon of the butter. Process until very smooth.

3. Return the spinach to the saucepan and add salt and freshly ground black pepper to taste. Heat gently and transfer to a warm bowl. Top with the remaining teaspoon of butter. Serve immediately.

Serves 4

# Green Beans
## Three Ways

### *Simple*

### Green Beans Almondine

*A simple dish that's loved by all.*

**450 g (1 lb) green beans**
**2 tablespoons unsalted butter**
**3 tablespoons sliced almonds**

1. Wash the beans and trim the ends. Using a small, sharp knife, cut the beans in thirds across the width. You may also leave the beans whole.

2. Choose a saucepan large enough to hold the beans comfortably. Add enough water to fill it by two-thirds and bring the water to the boil with a teaspoon of salt. Add the beans and cook for 3 to 4 minutes if you've cut them, and 5 to 6 minutes if you've left them whole. Drain them immediately into a colander. Pat dry with a paper towel.

3. Put the butter into the saucepan in which the beans were cooked and melt the butter over a medium heat. Add the almonds and cook for about 2 minutes, just until they take on some colour. Then add the drained beans and ½ a teaspoon of salt, and cook for another 2 minutes, tossing until the beans are coated with butter. Add freshly ground black pepper and serve.

Serves 4 or more

# Fun

## Green Beans with Pesto and Walnuts

*This is great to take to a picnic or pack in a lunch box.*

**450 g (1 lb) green beans**
**80 g (2½ oz) coarsely chopped walnut pieces**
**60 g (2 oz) good-quality pesto**

1. Trim the ends of the beans with a small, sharp knife. Cut the beans in half across the width. Set aside.

2. Bring a large pot of water, fitted with a steamer basket, to the boil. Place the beans in the steamer basket and cover. Steam for about 6 minutes until the beans are tender but still bright green.

3. Put the walnuts in a small nonstick frying pan over a medium-high heat for about 2 minutes, stirring constantly, until the nuts are lightly toasted. Sprinkle lightly with salt and set aside.

4. Put the pesto in a medium-sized bowl. When the beans are cooked, shake off any extra moisture and add the beans to the bowl with the pesto. Toss quickly and add the nuts. Add salt and freshly ground black pepper to taste, and stir. Serve hot or at room temperature.

Serves 4 or more

# Divine

## Green Beans with Bacon

*Roasting green beans at a high temperature makes them all wrinkled and very delicious.*

**450 g (1 lb) green beans, ends trimmed**
**1 tablespoon olive oil**
**4 slices of bacon**

1. Preheat the oven to 200°C (400°F/gas mark 6).

2. Wash the beans and dry. Toss with the olive oil and sprinkle with salt. Put the beans in one layer on a rimmed baking tray. Bake for 20 minutes, shaking the pan once or twice during this time to prevent sticking.

3. Meanwhile, cook the bacon in a skillet over a medium-high heat until just crispy. Drain on paper towels. Chop into small pieces.

4. After about 20 minutes, the green beans will be wrinkled and have golden-brown spots. Transfer to a large bowl or serving dish and sprinkle with salt and freshly ground black pepper. Toss well and scatter bacon on top. Serve hot or at room temperature.

Serves 4

# Roasted Rosemary
# Potatoes

*Rosemary is a potato's best friend.*

**700 g (1½ lb) Maris Piper potatoes**
**1 tablespoon finely chopped fresh rosemary**
**2½ tablespoons olive oil**

1. Preheat the oven to 200°C (400°F/gas mark 6).

2. Peel the potatoes and cut them into 2½-cm (1-in) chunks.
   Put them in a bowl. Add the rosemary, 2 tablespoons of
   the olive oil and 2 teaspoons of salt. Stir well to coat the
   potatoes thoroughly.

3. Drizzle the remaining ½ tablespoon of olive oil on a rimmed
   baking tray. Bake for 35 minutes, turning the potatoes with a
   spatula every 10 minutes. When the potatoes are crispy and
   tender, transfer them to a large plate. Sprinkle with salt.

Serves 4

# Creamy Potato Gratin

*You will feel like a great French chef when you make this classic recipe.*

**110 g (4 oz) Comté or Gruyere cheese**
**4 large baking potatoes – about 900 g (2 lb)**
**360 ml (12 fl oz) single cream**

1. Preheat the oven to 180°C (350°F/gas mark 4).

2. Grate the cheese on the large holes of a box grater. Set aside.

3. Peel the potatoes and cut across the width into very thin slices. Spray a 20 cm x 20-cm (8 x 8-in) glass baking dish or a small shallow casserole dish with cooking spray. Arrange one third of the slices, overlapping, in the bottom of the dish. Sprinkle with a ¼ teaspoon of salt and freshly ground black pepper. Cover with one third of the cheese.

4. Make 2 more layers of potatoes and cheese, sprinkling each layer with a ¼ teaspoon of salt and freshly ground black pepper.

5. Pour the cream over the top. Bake for 25 minutes and press the potatoes down firmly with a spatula. Cook for 25 minutes longer until golden brown.

Serves 6

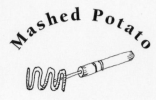

## Mashed Potato

## Extras

Bacon bits

Buttermilk

Chopped fresh herbs

Chopped spring onions

Creamed spinach

Crispy onions

Crumbled blue cheese

Grated Cheddar cheese

Gravy

Peas

Pesto

Roasted garlic

Sautéed mushrooms

Sautéed onions

Sour cream

Sun-dried tomatoes

Sweetcorn

Wasabi paste

# The Best Mashed Potatoes

*The best mashed potatoes are made with baking potatoes to which hot milk and cold butter are added. Yum!*

**5 baking potatoes – about 900 g (2 lb)**
**240 ml (8 fl oz) milk**
**6 tablespoons (75 g/3 oz) unsalted butter**

1. Peel the potatoes. Cut in half lengthwise and then crosswise. Place in a medium-sized saucepan with water to cover by 2½ cm (1 in). Add 1 tablespoon of salt and bring to a rapid boil. Cover the pan and cook over a medium heat for 25 minutes, or until the potatoes are tender. Remove potatoes from the pan with a slotted spoon and place them in a colander in the sink. Pat dry and put them in a large bowl.

2. Put the milk in a small saucepan and bring just to the boil. Lower the heat and cook for 1 minute.

3. Using a potato masher, mash the potatoes, slowly adding the hot milk. Add small bits of butter and continue to mash until they reach the desired consistency. Some people like them lumpy; others like them smooth. Add salt and freshly ground black pepper to taste.

Serves 6

Marvellous mashed potatoes
make a meal memorable!

# Sweet Potato Wedges
# with Maple Syrup

*This is an unexpectedly delicious treat for a party.*

**2 large sweet potatoes, 225 g (8 oz) each**
**2 tablespoons vegetable oil**
**4¼ tablespoons maple syrup**

1. Preheat the oven to 190°C (375°F/gas mark 5).

2. Peel the sweet potatoes using a vegetable peeler. Cut each into 8 long wedges. The best way to do this is to cut the potatoes in half lengthwise and then slice each half into 4 long wedges.

3. Put the sweet potatoes in a bowl. Add the oil and toss until the potatoes are coated with oil. Place them on a rimmed baking tray with the pointed side up.

4. Roast for 15 minutes, then turn the potatoes on another side. Bake for 8 minutes longer and turn the potatoes on their third side. Then bake for about 7 minutes longer. The potatoes should be tender when pierced with a sharp knife. Total cooking time is about 30 minutes. Transfer the potatoes to a serving dish. Sprinkle with salt and freshly ground black pepper and drizzle with the maple syrup.

Serves 4

# Creative Coconut Rice

*The first two ingredients are fragrant basmati rice and light coconut milk. The third ingredient is up to you! Each suggestion takes your taste buds in a new direction. Try them all and tell me which one you like best!*

**225 g (8 oz) basmati rice**
**240 ml (8 fl oz) coconut milk**
**1 tablespoon unsalted butter OR**
**35 g (1¼ oz) finely chopped pistachios OR**
**½ teaspoon curry powder, or more to taste**

1. Put the rice, coconut milk, 240 ml (8 fl oz) of water and 1 teaspoon of salt in a large saucepan with a lid. Bring to the boil, stirring once. Reduce the heat to very low, cover the saucepan, and simmer for 18 minutes, stirring once or twice during cooking. Remove from the heat and let stand covered for 5 minutes, or until all the liquid is absorbed.

2. Prepare the third ingredient. If using pistachios, put them in a small nonstick frying pan and stir constantly over a medium-high heat until they are lightly browned.

3. Add the butter or pistachios or curry powder to the hot rice. Add salt and freshly ground white pepper to taste. Stir and serve.

Serves 4 or more

Dessert
Menu

# Heavenly Chocolate Mousse Cake

*The name of the cake says it all! It is warm, rich, moist and flourless.*

**450 g (1 lb) plain cooking chocolate**
**10 tablespoons (175 g/6 oz) unsalted butter**
**5 large eggs**

1. Preheat the oven to 190°C (375°F/gas mark 5).

2. Line the bottom of a 20-cm (8-in) springform cake tin with a circle of greaseproof paper or silver foil. Spray the inside of the pan with cooking spray.

3. Chop the chocolate into pieces if necessary. Cut the butter into small chunks. Place the chocolate and butter in a bowl over a saucepan of simmering water. Heat, stirring constantly, until the chocolate has melted and the mixture is smooth. Let it cool.

4. Using an electric mixer, beat the eggs with a pinch of salt. Beat at high speed for about 5 minutes until the mixture is very thick and increases in volume. Slowly pour the chocolate mixture into the beaten eggs and mix gently until the chocolate is thoroughly incorporated. Pour the mixture into the prepared tin. Bake for 22 minutes.

4. Remove from the oven. The centre will still be soft. Let it cool for at least 45 minutes. (You can refrigerate the cake for up to 2 days; let it sit at room temperature for several hours before serving.)

Serves 8

The name says it all...

# Chocolate Banana Terrine

*This is even better than birthday cake and requires no baking! It looks like a loaf and the French call it a terrine. Just add candles!*

**5 small bananas**
**240 ml (8 fl oz) double cream**
**450 g (16 oz) milk or plain cooking chocolate**

1. Line a 20 × 10-cm (8 × 4-in) loaf tin with cling film so that it overhangs the edges by 7½ cm (3 in). Place the bananas in the pan to make 2 layers, trimming the ends so that the bananas easily fit into the pan.

2. In a small saucepan, heat the cream over a medium heat until hot, but not boiling. Add the chocolate and heat, stirring constantly, until the chocolate is completely melted and the mixture is smooth. Pour the chocolate mixture over the bananas. You want the chocolate to seep between the layers. Tap the pan down several times to release any air bubbles. Let it cool. Loosely fold the cling film over the top of the terrine. Refrigerate overnight or until the terrine is very firm.

3. Fold back the cling film. Turn the tin upside down on a bread board to unmould. Lift the tin from the terrine. Remove the cling film and cut into thick slices.

Serves 8 or more

# Warm Banana Tart

*According to Danielle Hartog, my 11-year-old sous-chef, this recipe will make you feel like a professional chef.*

**1 sheet frozen puff pastry – about 225 g (8 oz)**
**8 tablespoons apricot jam**
**3 ripe medium-sized bananas**

1. Preheat the oven to 190°C (375°F/gas mark 5).

2. Thaw the pastry according to package directions. While the pastry is cold but bendable, roll it out with a rolling pin to stretch the dough 6 mm (¼ in) longer and 6 mm (¼ in) wider. Cut the dough into quarters so that you have 4 rectangles. Leaving a 6-mm (¼-in) border on each side of the rectangle, prick the pastry (except the edges) all over with the prongs of a fork.

3. Put the jam and 2 tablespoons of water into a small saucepan. Stir over a medium heat until the jam is melted and smooth.

4. Peel the bananas and slice thinly. Arrange the bananas in a tight overlapping pattern to completely cover the pastry, but not the edges. Using a pastry brush, brush the warm jam over the bananas (do not let it drip on the edges of the pastry). Place the tarts on an ungreased baking tray and bake for 25 minutes, or until golden. Lightly brush the bananas with the remaining melted jam. Let them cool.

Serves 4

'I loved making the banana tarts because they looked sooo professional when they were done.' —Danielle Hartog, aged 11

# Strawberries in Nightgowns

*Here, melted chocolate covers big bright strawberries with a shiny chocolate coating that hardens as it sits. You can dip the dark chocolate strawberries into coconut flakes and the white chocolate strawberries into chocolate sprinkles. Or do it the other way around! Either way they are delicious and look beautiful, too!*

**16 to 20 large ripe strawberries – about 450 g (1 lb)**
**175 g (6 oz) plain or white cooking chocolate chips**
**55 g (2 oz) chocolate sprinkles (sometimes called**
**vermicelli or strands) or flaked coconut**

1. Wash the strawberries and pat completely dry. This is an important step. Leave the green stems on for easy dipping.

2. Put the plain or white chocolate chips in a bowl over a saucepan of simmering water. Let the chocolate slowly melt until it is completely smooth, stirring occasionally. Remove from the heat.

3. One by one, dip each strawberry into the mixture. Cover each one with a thin coating three-quarters of the way up and shake any excess off. You want to leave a band of red showing at the top. Let dry for 1 minute.

4. Line a large plate with greaseproof paper. Put sprinkles or coconut in a shallow bowl. Dip each strawberry lightly in the sprinkles or coconut to lightly coat. Place on the greaseproof paper. Let the chocolate cool and harden. It is best to eat these the same day they are made.

'Strawberries-in-Nightgowns were my favourite. My younger brother Daniel said they were awesome. I even tried dipping slices of clementine oranges in the chocolate mixture and called them Tangy Tops. They were delicious.'

–Rachel Greenberg, aged 12

Makes 16–20

# Strawberries with Mint Sugar

*You will love the bold flavours of ripe red strawberries under a blanket of green-flecked snow. Think of other ways to use this mint-flavoured sugar. I like it sprinkled on grapefruit, or you might add it to a glass of iced tea.*

**1 litre (2 pints) ripe strawberries**
**75 g (2½ oz) sugar**
**1 bunch fresh mint**

1. Wash the strawberries and dry well. Remove the green stems. Cut the strawberries in half lengthwise and place in a pretty bowl.

2. Put the sugar in the bowl of a food processor. Wash the mint and dry very well. Make sure there is absolutely no water on the mint. Remove all the mint leaves. Using a knife on a chopping board, coarsely chop enough mint leaves to get 7½ g (¼ oz). Add to the sugar and process until the mint is mixed into the sugar.

3. Sprinkle the mint sugar all over the berries and serve immediately. Garnish with a few whole leaves of remaining mint.

Serves 4

One should never turn down
the chance to make fondue!

# Fresh Cherries with Chocolate Fondue

*Fresh cherries are the ideal fruit for this recipe because they come with stems for easy dipping and pair especially well with chocolate. You may use chocolate chips, chunks or bars.*

**450 g (1 lb) fresh red cherries with stems**

**180 ml (6 fl oz) light coconut milk**

**175 g (6 oz) plain cooking chocolate, chopped into small pieces if using a bar**

1. Wash the cherries and dry with a paper towel. Do not remove the stems. Chill until ready to serve.

2. Pour the coconut milk into a small, heavy saucepan. Cook over a medium heat until hot. Add the chocolate to the hot coconut milk. Reduce the heat to low and cook, stirring constantly, until the chocolate melts and the mixture is very smooth.

3. Transfer the mixture to a small fondue pot or a soufflé dish. Serve with the cherries for dipping.

Serves 4

*This fondue is also fabulous with other fruit:*

- fresh orange segments, banana chunks, or wedges of apple or pear

- sponge cake, sponge fingers, shortbread or biscotti (Italian biscuits)

# Chocolate Sandwich Biscuits

*Be sure to use self-raising flour for these brownie-like biscuits.*

**260 g (9 oz) Nutella**
**1 large egg**
**145 g (5 oz) self-raising flour**

1. Preheat the oven to 190°C (375°F/gas mark 5).

2. Put half the Nutella and the egg into the bowl of an electric mixer. Mix well. Slowly add 115 g (4 oz) of the flour until a wet dough is formed. Dust a clean board or worktop with the remaining 30 g (1 oz) of flour and transfer the dough to the board. Knead gently until a smooth dough forms; the dough will be a little sticky. Roll the dough into 18 balls, flouring your hands as you go to make rolling easier. Place the balls on a greaseproof-lined baking tray, well spaced apart.

3. Bake for 10 to 12 minutes and remove from the oven. Allow them to cool for 10 minutes. Using a serrated knife, cut the biscuits in half horizontally. Spread the bottom with 1 teaspoon of the remaining Nutella and replace the top, pressing firmly. Let them cool. Store in a tightly covered tin.

Makes 18

# Simple Butter Biscuits

*These belong in biscuit tins everywhere. They are buttery and very soft.*

**200 g (7 oz) unsalted butter at
room temperature**

**125 g (4½ oz) icing sugar, plus more for dusting**

**225 g (8 oz) plain flour,
plus more for dusting the board**

1. Preheat the oven to 150°C (300°F/gas mark 2).

2. Put the butter in the bowl of an electric mixer. Beat the butter until light and fluffy. You may also use a hand-held mixer. Add the sugar gradually and beat well. Stir in the flour and add a large pinch of salt. Continue to mix on low until a smooth ball of dough is formed.

3. Sprinkle the worktop lightly with flour. Using a rolling pin, roll out the dough about 6 mm (¼ in) thick. Cut out the biscuits using any decorative cookie cutter you desire: I like to use 5-cm (2-in) round fluted cookie cutters. Or cut out the numbers 1-2-3 using number cookie cutters; or make stars or half-moon shapes.

4. Bake on an ungreased baking tray for about 25 minutes, or until the biscuits are dry and pale in colour. Remove from the baking tray only when the biscuits have cooled. Dust the biscuits with additional icing sugar shaken through a coarse-mesh sieve.

Makes 36 to 40 biscuits

# Iced Strawberry Tea

*This will become one of your favourite thirst-quenchers. Great for a tea party, serve this fabulous iced tea with a big plate of Simple Butter Biscuits.*

**450 g (1 lb) strawberries,
plus more for garnish**

**110 g (4 oz) sugar**

**2 Assam tea bags**

1. Wash the strawberries and remove the stems. Cut the strawberries in half, put in the bowl of a food processor with the sugar, and process until very smooth.

2. Bring 960 ml (32 fl oz) of water to the boil. Pour the water into a large heatproof jar, add the tea bags and let steep for 5 minutes.

3. Combine the strawberry purée with the tea. Strain through a coarse-mesh strainer into a jug. Let it cool. Cover and refrigerate until very cold.

4. Serve over ice with additional strawberries as a garnish.

Serves 6

Let the night-time oven
do its magic.

# Biscuits While You Sleep

*Put glossy heaps of wet meringue into the oven before bedtime
and in the morning you will wake up to dreamy crisp biscuits.*

**3 large egg whites**
**195 g (7 oz) sugar**
**175 g (6 oz) mini chocolate chips**

1. Preheat the oven to 190°C (375°F/gas mark 5).

2. Beat the egg whites in the bowl of an electric mixer until
   they just begin to thicken. Add a pinch of salt and gradually
   add the sugar. Beat for several minutes until the mixture
   holds it shape and is stiff and glossy.

3. Line 2 rimmed baking trays with greaseproof paper. Gently
   fold the chocolate chips into the meringue mixture and
   drop by the tablespoonful on to the baking trays. Place in
   the oven on the middle rack and turn the oven off immediately. Leave the door closed until morning. Sweet dreams!

Makes about 28

'For the Chocolate Pecan Fudge we bought prechopped pecans and that saved time. We had half a tin of the condensed milk left, so we just doubled the recipe and made a bigger batch. It was fantastic.'

*–Ben Deem, aged 10*

# Chocolate Pecan Fudge

*This is a yummy little treat you can whip up easily. Great for kids – and adults, too!*

**115 g (4 oz) coarsely chopped pecans**
**320 ml (11 fl oz) condensed milk**
**350 g (12 oz) plain chocolate chips**

1. Place the pecans in a small nonstick frying pan and add a large pinch of salt. Cook over a medium heat, stirring constantly, until the nuts are toasted. Set aside to cool.

2. Put the condensed milk in a small saucepan. Heat until it just comes to the boil. Add the chocolate and immediately reduce the heat to low. Continue to cook, stirring constantly, until the chocolate has melted and the mixture is smooth. Stir in the pecans until well blended.

3. Line a 20 x 20-cm (8 x 8-in) square pan with cling film so that 10 cm (4 in) hang over the sides of the pan. Pour the mixture into the pan and cover with the panels of cling film. Refrigerate until cold. Cut into small squares. Let sit at room temperature before serving.

Makes 16 pieces

# Lemon and Buttermilk Sorbet

*This is awesome. It's creamy, lemony and sweet. Delicious on top of a mound of berries!*

**450 g (1 lb) sugar**
**4 large lemons**
**1 litre buttermilk**

1. Put the sugar in a large bowl. Wash the lemons and dry them. Grate the zest of 3 lemons and add to the sugar. Cut all the lemons in half and squeeze to get 120 ml (4 fl oz) of juice. Add the juice to the sugar and stir with a wooden spoon until the mixture is smooth.

2. Whisk in the buttermilk and a pinch of salt. Stir until sugar is dissolved. Cover and chill for several hours or overnight.

3. Freeze in an ice-cream maker according to the manufacturer's directions.

Serves 8

# Orange Sundae

*This dessert – freshly-made orange ice cream with orange caramel sauce – looks especially delicious when served in a big scooped-out orange instead of a bowl.*

**360 ml (12 fl oz) single cream**
**225 g (8 oz) sugar**
**840 ml (28 fl oz) freshly squeezed orange juice**

1. Put the single cream in a large saucepan with 165 g (7 oz) of the sugar and a pinch of salt. Bring just to the boil, whisking constantly. Remove from the heat and let it cool. Add 720 ml (24 fl oz) of the orange juice to the mixture and whisk until blended. Cover and refrigerate until very cold. Freeze in an ice-cream maker according to the manufacturer's directions.

2. Make orange caramel sauce by placing the remaining 60 g (2 oz) of sugar in a small nonstick frying pan. Cook over a medium-high heat, stirring constantly with a wooden spoon, until the sugar turns into a dark clear liquid. Carefully add the remaining 120 ml (4 fl oz) of orange juice; remember, this is very hot. The mixture will bubble up and harden, but continue to cook it over a high heat until the hardened sugar melts. **Be sure to do this step with an adult.** Continue to cook until the sauce is reduced to 6 tablespoons. Let it cool.

3. Serve the ice cream in dessert dishes or in big scooped-out oranges. Pour the sauce on top.

Serves 4

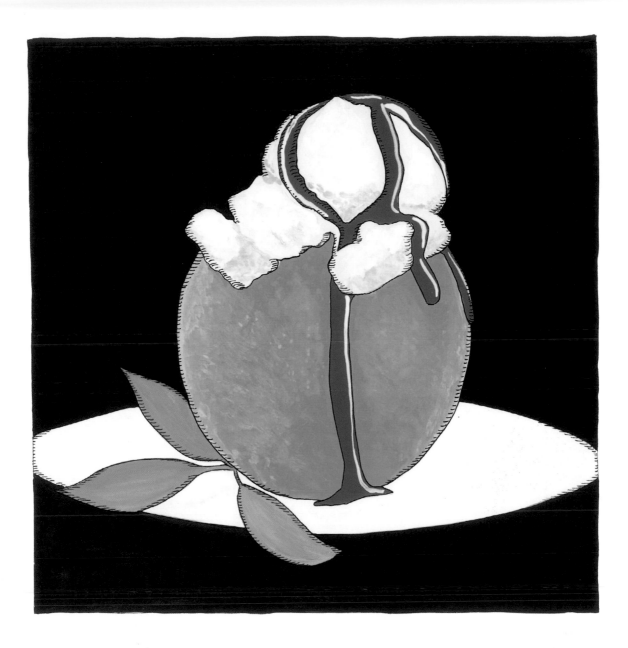

Amaze your friends and family
(no one has to know how simple it was!)

# Watermelon Ices with Chocolate Chips

*The riper the watermelon, the more delicious this tastes. Watermelon and chocolate taste great together.*

**600 g (21 oz) diced ripe watermelon**
**165 g (6 oz) sugar**
**85 g (3 oz) mini chocolate chips**

1. Remove the seeds from the watermelon. Put the watermelon in the bowl of a food processor and process until very smooth. Add the sugar and a pinch of salt and continue to process until the sugar is dissolved.

2. Transfer the mixture to a metal pie dish and place in the freezer. After 30 minutes, using a fork, break up the ice crystals so that they are of uniform size. Continue to break up ice crystals every hour until the mixture is frozen – about 3 hours.

3. When ready to serve, chill the bowl and blade of a food processor. Break the frozen mixture into chunks and place in the chilled bowl. Process until very smooth. Spoon the ice into chilled glasses and sprinkle with chocolate chips. Serve immediately.

Serves 4

# Quick Ice Cream Sauces . . .

## made from ice cream!

## Maple and Walnut Sauce

*Sous-chef Ben Deem didn't think he would like this at all, but after making it he thought it was fabulous!*

**6 tablespoons maple syrup**
**120 ml (4 fl oz) vanilla ice cream**
**40 g (1½ oz) chopped walnuts**

Put the maple syrup and a pinch of salt in a small saucepan. Bring to the boil, then lower the heat to medium. Continue to cook for about 5 minutes, not stirring, until the syrup reduces a little and thickens. Using a wire whisk, add in the ice cream until completely smooth, cooking 1 minute longer. Remove from the heat and stir in the walnuts. Serve immediately or reheat gently before serving.

## Hot Fudge

When cold, this makes a great icing for cupcakes. When hot, it turns a simple scoop of ice cream into something special.

**180 ml (6 fl oz) vanilla ice cream**
**225 g (8 oz) chocolate chips**
**2 tablespoons golden syrup**

Put the ice cream in a small, heavy saucepan over a medium heat. Let it melt and then bring just to the boil. Add the chocolate, then immediately lower the heat. Stir constantly until the sauce is smooth. Add the golden syrup and cook for 1 minute, stirring constantly. Serve immediately or reheat before serving.

'The hot fudge was really easy to make. It was like the really gooey warm fudge you'd find in an ice-cream shop.'

–Ben Deem, aged 10

# Index

# Acknowledgements

What a joy having my readers help create this book! I couldn't have done it without a brigade of sous-chefs who diligently tested the recipes and shared their tasting notes and comments. They included: Danielle Hartog, aged 11; Ian Kimmel, aged 12; Robyn Kimmel, aged 8; Daniel Glass, aged 11; Sara Rosen, aged 16; Benjamin Deem, aged 10; Rachel Greenberg, aged 12; Philip Safran, aged 10; Nicolas Green, aged 11; and Julia Miller, aged 11. Devoted tasters included: Max Deem, aged 12; Daniel Greenberg, aged 10; Sara Feld, aged 15; and my equally enthusiastic and ageless husband, Michael Whiteman.

Danielle, whom I met quite accidentally at Kitchen Arts and Letters, a New York City 'sweet shop' of cookbooks, wins the title of 'executive sous-chef'. She has what it takes to be a culinary star. Thanks also go to her wonderful mum, Cindy Hartog.

Creativity abounds among Victoria Arms, Liz Schonhorst and Deb Shapiro at Bloomsbury, where all things are possible. Thanks to Sara Pinto, whose whimsical illustrations touch your heart, and to Norman Weinstein, who honed my knife skills.

Thank you to my beautiful mother, Marion Gold. I still tug at her apron strings and love her more than words can say. To the memory of my father, Bill Gold, who got me hooked on the pleasures of food at a very early age. To my brother, Leon Gold, who broke all the rules with tuna fish sandwiches and watermelon for breakfast. To his wife, Gail, a wonderful cook in her own right. To Amy Silverman, now Berkowitz, my best friend since 1966. And to Jeremy Whiteman, the best 'kid' of all.

*Rozanne Gold, a few years ago*

*Rozanne Gold, now*